PREDICTING THE MARKETS

Stock Buybacks:
The True Story

Edward Yardeni
Joseph Abbott

YRI PRESS

Edward Yardeni is President of Yardeni Research, Inc.
Joseph Abbott is the firm's Chief Quantitative Strategist

Predicting the Markets Topical Study #2:
Stock Buybacks: The True Story

Copyright © 2019 Edward Yardeni

ISBN: 978-1-948025-04-1 (paperback)
ISBN: 978-1-948025-05-8 (eBook)

The authors have taken all reasonable steps to provide accurate information in this publication. However, no representation or warranty is made as to the fairness, accuracy, completeness, or correctness of the information and opinions contained herein. Over time, the statements made in this publication may no longer be accurate, true, or otherwise correct. Over time, the authors' opinions as articulated in this publication may change. This publication should not be relied on for investment, accounting, legal, or other professional advice. If readers desire such advice, they should consult with a qualified professional. Nothing in this publication—including predictions, forecasts, and estimates for all markets—should be construed as recommendations to buy, sell, or hold any security, including mutual funds, futures contracts, exchange-traded funds, or any other financial instruments.

Published by YRI Press, a division of Yardeni Research, Inc.
68 Wheatley Road, Suite 1100
Brookville, New York 11545

Contact us: **requests@yardeni.com**

Note to Readers

These Topical Studies examine issues,
which were discussed in my book,
Predicting the Markets: A Professional Autobiography (2018),
but in greater detail and on a more current basis.
Other studies in this series can be found at
www.yardenibook.com/studies.

The charts included at the end
of this study were current as of July 2019.
Updates (in color) are also available at
www.yardenibook.com/studies.

Institutional investors are welcome
to sign up for our research service on a
four-week complimentary basis at
www.yardeni.com/trial-registration.

Introduction

Progressive politicians have pounced on corporate share buybacks lately. They see buybacks as a major source of income and wealth inequality, subpar capital spending, and lackluster productivity. In their opinion, buybacks have contributed greatly to the stagnation of the standards of living of most Americans in recent years. So they want to limit buybacks or even ban them.

Wall Street's stock market bears have been growling about buybacks as well. They've been arguing that buybacks have rigged the stock market in favor of the bulls. They claim that the buybacks have been mostly financed with debt. As a result, corporate balance sheets have become increasingly leveraged, which makes them vulnerable to a recession and likely would exacerbate any economic downturn. The bears therefore remain bearish and expect to be vindicated with a vengeance, eventually.

The facts don't support the narratives of either the Progressives in Washington or the bears on Wall Street. The true story is hiding in plain sight. The most common reason that S&P 500 companies buy back their shares is to offset the dilution in the number of shares outstanding that results when employee compensation takes the form of stock options and stock grants that vest over time, not just for top executives but for many employees. In effect, the ultimate source of funds for most stock buybacks is the employee compensation expense item on corporate income statements, not bond issuance as the bears contend.

To a large extent, the bull market in stocks has been boosting buybacks, rather than the other way around as widely believed. Rising stock prices increase the attractiveness of paying some of employees' compensation with stock grants. Buybacks then are necessary to offset the dilution of earnings per share.

Like previous bull markets, the latest one has been driven by rising earnings, but earnings have not been boosted artificially and significantly on a per-share basis by stock buybacks, as widely perceived. Nevertheless, buybacks might have provided a lift to stock prices, since the buybacks occur in the open market, while the issuance of stock as compensation has no immediate market impact, especially if not yet vested or exercised.

As for the Progressives' narrative, there is no evidence that buybacks per se have worsened income inequality. Stock compensation clearly has boosted the incomes of plenty of corporate executives, but that stems from the bull market in stocks since 2009 more than from buybacks. More importantly, blaming buy-backs for widespread income stagnation doesn't make any sense, since the data clearly show that standards of living have been rising in record-high territory for most Americans for several years, contrary to the Progressives' tale of widespread woe.

Government Is Here to Help

Journalist H.L. Mencken famously observed: "The whole aim of practical politics is to keep the populace alarmed (and hence clamorous to be led to safety) by menacing it with an endless series of hobgoblins, all of them imaginary." Ronald Reagan just as famously warned: "The nine most terrifying words in the English language are 'I'm from the government, and I'm here to help.'"

Rahm Emanuel summed it all up neatly when he said: "You never want a serious crisis to go to waste. And what I mean by that is an opportunity to do things that you think you could not do before." The corollary of Rahm's Law is that the government tends to cre-ate crises so that we will need more government to fix them. A case in point is stock buybacks. Consider the following:

Senators Schumer and Sanders want to limit buybacks. Senators Chuck Schumer (D-NY) and Bernie Sanders (D-VT), who is running for president, long for the good old days. They believe that our nation's glory days can be restored by limiting corporate stock buybacks. They said so in a February 3, 2019 op-ed for *The New York Times.*[1] According to the two senators, the period from the 1950s through the 1970s was a golden age for workers because "American corporations shared a belief that they had a duty not only to their shareholders but to their workers, their communities and the country that created the economic conditions and legal protections for them to thrive."

However, in recent decades, corporate managements and their boards of directors have become greedy, focusing on maximizing "shareholders' earnings" at the expense of workers' earnings. The result has been the "worst level of income inequality in decades," they claim.

As proof, they offer the "explosion of stock buybacks." From 2008 through 2017, corporations boosted their earnings per share and the value of their stocks by spending close to 100% of their profits on buybacks (53%) and dividends (40%)—which the senators characterize as corporate "self-indulgence." They bemoan that

---

1 "Schumer and Sanders: Limit Corporate Stock Buybacks," *The New York Times,* February 3, 2019.

corporations haven't been investing enough to strengthen their businesses or boost the productivity of their workers. So, they say, stock-holding managements have gotten richer at the expense of workers who don't hold stock and haven't benefitted from rising stock prices—thus exacerbating both income and wealth inequality. Adding insult to injury, "the median wages of average workers have remained relatively stagnant." While the corporate fat cats are getting fatter on buybacks, workers "get handed a pink slip."

The two senators, who have never managed any business, intend to fix this problem. They are planning to introduce a bill that will prohibit any corporation from buying back its shares unless it first provides a minimum wage of $15 an hour and a basic package of employee benefits, which presumably the bill will spell out. The senators recognize that corporations would respond by paying out more in dividends if they can't buy back their shares. They promise more legislation to deal with that issue if necessary, maybe by amending the tax code.

Senator Baldwin wants to ban most buybacks. On March 26, 2019, Senator Tammy Baldwin (D-WI) released a report arguing that stock buybacks suppress wages and drive income inequality while increasing systemic risk to the economy. One of the alarming findings is that the "evidence also shows that Wall Street insiders and corporate executives have abused the American system of corporate governance, spending trillions on buybacks to benefit themselves at the expense of employees and other corporate stakeholders." Baldwin's report, *Reward Work Not Wealth,* is subtitled *"A Plan to Reform Corporate Governance, Empower Workers and End the Looting of Public Companies to Create Shared Prosperity in America."*[2]

Baldwin wants to ban open-market stock repurchases and is reintroducing the Reward Work Act in the 116th Congress, which she had first introduced a year ago. In addition to prohibiting such buybacks, her bill requires that one-third of the directors of each public company be elected by its employees. It would be a radical intrusion by the government into corporate finance and governance.

The report claims that "the buyback binge" has been financed by "risky" debt to buy back shares, and declares: "This dynamic has pushed corporate debt to record highs. The share-sellers reap short-term gains, yet they bear none of the risks of the other stakeholders, who are left to face the prospect of a default. Long-term

---

2   *Reward Work Not Wealth: A Plan to Reform Corporate Governance, Empower Workers and End the Looting of Public Companies to Create Shared Prosperity in America,* Office of Tammy Baldwin, U.S. Senator of Wisconsin.

retirement savers suffer the permanent loss of their investment if the company goes bankrupt. Workers face the loss of their job and pension cuts, possibly resulting in a delayed retirement. Taxpayers deal with further strain on public resources when they are used to assist workers who lose their jobs."

In a similar vein, Gluskin Sheff Chief Economist and Strategist David Rosenberg recently warned that the next recession will be exacerbated by the deterioration in corporate balance sheets caused by buybacks. In a May 5, 2019 CNBC interview, he said: "I don't think it's going to be a deep recession, and it's not about the consumers or housing or the banks. It's really about these bloated corporate balance sheets. There will be a price to pay for the unprecedented debt-for-equity swap we did this cycle, borrowing at low interest rates and buying back your stock. That is certainly something that is not sustainable."[3]

A Nagging Doubt

One of the main reasons I have been bullish during the current bull market is the proliferation of corporate stock

---

3   "Corporate buybacks will fuel the next recession and it could happen this year, says Wall Street bear," CNBC, May 5, 2019.

buybacks. Early on in the bull market, the bears argued that stock prices were on a "sugar high" and "running on fumes." They claimed that the economy remained weak and vulnerable to another recession. Earnings, they contended, were boosted by cost-cutting without much help from revenues. I argued that the economy was recovering and so were revenues and earnings. The bears countered that the data showed that neither individual nor institutional investors were buying stocks, which meant that stock prices couldn't continue to rally.

I argued that the mounting pace of stock buybacks confirmed that corporations were the big buyers of their own shares. I attributed this development to rising profits and cash flow and a significant spread between the forward earnings yield of the S&P 500 and the after-tax cost of borrowing money in the corporate bond market (Fig. 1). In a sense, this spread revived the Fed's Stock Valuation Model, but as a corporate finance model rather than as a stocks-vs-bonds asset allocation model. I showed that there was a strong correlation between the S&P 500 stock price index and the sum of S&P 500 buybacks and dividends.

It was a simple analysis of what was driving the bull market, and it worked very well for me. However, along the way, I had one major nagging doubt about this model: There wasn't much difference between the growth rates of S&P 500 earnings on a per-share basis and in aggregate. Surely if corporations were buying back their shares to the tune of several hundred billion dollars per year, the former should grow measurably faster than the latter. That wasn't happening and didn't support the widespread view—which remains widespread—that the whole point of buybacks is to increase *earnings per share* to drive up stock prices. I knew that buybacks must be bullish, but that belief wasn't confirmed by the relatively narrow spread between the growth rates of per-share and aggregate earnings.

The *Financial Accounts of the United States*, compiled quarterly by the Fed, has data for nonfinancial corporations that seemed to corroborate my simple model and the now-widespread view that the activity of corporate repurchasers has driven the bull market, not the activity of investors.[4] Indeed, the data backed up the basic premise of a February 25, 2019 article in *The New York Times* by financial reporter Matt Phillips titled "This Stock Market Rally Has Everything, Except Investors."[5] Here is the introduction of the piece:

> Armchair investors have been selling stock. So have pension funds and mutual funds, as well as a whole other category of investors—nonprofit

4   *Financial Accounts of the United States,* Board of Governors of the Financial Reserve System, December 6, 2018.

5   "This Stock Market Rally Has Everything, Except Investors," *The New York Times*, February 25, 2019.

groups, endowments, private equity firms and personal trusts. The stock market is off to its best start since 1987, but these investors are expected to dump hundreds of billions of dollars of shares this year. So who is pushing prices higher? In part, the companies themselves. American corporations flush with cash from last year's tax cuts and a growing economy are buying back their own shares at an extraordinary clip. They have good reason: Buybacks allow them to return cash to shareholders, burnish key measures of financial performance and goose their share prices. The surge in buybacks reflects a fundamental shift in how the market is operating, cementing the position of corporations as the single largest source of demand for American stocks.

That's exactly the story I've been telling during the bull market. It's now the consensus view, as evidenced by the article in *The New York Times,* which was based partly on flow-of-funds projections by Goldman Sachs. All the more reason to question the underlying premise of the now-consensus view of buybacks. The urgency of getting to the true story has been heightened by the sudden interest of politicians to regulate, if not ban, buybacks.

Original Sin and Redemption

Where shall I start to expose the weak foundations of the senators' arguments? I'll begin at the beginning:

SEC eases the rules on buybacks. Not widely known is that for many years after the Great Crash of 1929, the Securities and Exchange Commission (SEC) viewed buybacks as bordering on criminal activity. That was the case up until the Reagan years, when the SEC began to ease the rules on buybacks under John Shad, chairman from 1981 to 1987. He believed that the deregulation of securities markets would be good for the economy. In 1982, the SEC adopted Rule 10b-18, which provided a "safe harbor" for companies to do buybacks.[6]

In a widely read September 2014 *Harvard Business Review* article titled "Profits Without Prosperity," William Lazonick, a professor of economics at the University of Massachusetts, argued that buybacks are effectively a form of stock price manipulation.[7] In a recent interview, he called them "a license to loot."[8] Lazonick's buybacks-are-bad spin has been a big hit with progressive

---

6   For more, see "Rule 10b-18," Investopedia, April 15, 2019.

7   William Lazonick, "Profits Without Prosperity," *Harvard Business Review,* September 2014.

8   "Have Stock Buybacks Gone Too Far?" Knowledge @ Wharton, May 14, 2019.

politicians like Senator Elizabeth Warren (D-MA), who is running for president.

Bill Clinton inadvertently boosts stock compensation for top execs. Granted, some corporate executives are paid too much and spend too much time boosting their stock prices—purportedly under the banner of "enhancing shareholder value." They claim that high compensation and rising stock prices incent them (since most of them are shareholders) to work hard to manage their companies very well.

Ironically, many executives became even bigger shareholders after President Bill Clinton changed the tax code in 1993, when he signed into law his first budget, creating Section 162(m) of the Internal Revenue Code. This provision placed a $1 million limit on the amount that corporations could treat as a tax-deductible expense for compensation paid to the top five executives. Later this was changed by the SEC under President George W. Bush to the top four execs. It was hoped that would put an end to skyrocketing executive pay.

The law of unintended consequences trumped the new tax provision, which had a huge flaw—it exempted "performance-based" pay, such as stock options, from the $1 million cap. Businesses started paying executives more in stock options, and top executive pay continued to soar. Liberal critics, notably Senator Warren, concluded that the 1993 tax-code change had backfired badly and that soaring executive pay has exacerbated income inequality.

Buybacks don't boost earnings per share significantly. The widely believed notion that buybacks boost earnings per share by reducing the share count isn't supported by the data Standard & Poor's provides for the S&P 500 companies. While S&P 500 companies repurchased a whopping $4.7 trillion of their shares from the first quarter of 2009 through the fourth quarter of 2018, the spread between the growth rates in S&P 500 earnings per share and aggregate S&P 500 earnings has been tiny since the start of the available data during the fourth quarter of 1994, as Joe and I show below.

The best explanation for this surprising development is that the S&P 500 companies, for the most part, repurchase their shares to offset the dilution in the number of shares outstanding that results from compensation paid in the form of stocks. It's not just top executives who are compensated in company stock but many other employees too.

Buybacks are not designed "to return cash to shareholders," as widely believed. While dividends are paid directly to investors, most buybacks don't have any direct impact on investors if they result in equities getting purchased in the open market to offset stocks distributed to employees. Those shifts from unconstrained sellers to constrained buyers (who can't sell until their stock grants vest) arguably have a net bullish impact that indirectly benefits all investors.

Buybacks shouldn't be compared to profits. The cost of buying back shares for the purpose of offsetting the obligations of employee stock grants is reflected for repurchasers in the compensation-related expense in calculating profits.

A February 2008 *BEA Briefing* titled "Employee Stock Options and the National Economic Accounts" reported: "In December 2004, the Financial Accounting Standards Board (FASB) issued a new standard—FAS-123R—for companies that requires them to value employee stock options ... using a fair-value-based method at the time they are granted and to record this value on financial reports as a compensation expense over the period of vesting."[9]

A March 2011 *BEA Briefing* titled "Comparing NIPA Profits with S&P 500 Profits" observed: "NIPA [National Income & Product Accounts] accounting and tax accounting have always treated employee stock options as an expense only when (and if) options are exercised. It is an operating expense and therefore always a cost

9   "Employee Stock Options and the National Economic Accounts,"
    BEA Briefing, February 2008.

deduction in the NIPA profits calculation."[10] Before the FASB standard became effective for calendar-year companies on January 1, 2006, "GAAP option expense reporting was completely at a company's discretion and reported as a nonoperating expense or, often, not reported at all. Since 2006, options grant expense was mandated by GAAP. It was included in the Standard & Poor's reporting starting in 2006 as an operating profits deduction." (See Appendix 1: Excerpts from BEA Briefings on Expensing of Stock Options.)

So: It makes no sense to compare the amount that S&P 500 corporations spend on buybacks to their after-tax profits, as is often done! In the NIPA, money spent on buybacks (to cover employee stock plan obligations) doesn't come out of the after-tax profits pool as dividend payouts and capital outlays do. The contention that money used for buybacks would be better invested in growth of the business is faulty.

In the NIPA, dividend distributions, on the other hand, do come out of after-tax profits, leaving undistributed profits. These undistributed profits, along with cash flow from the depreciation allowance, can be spent on capital outlays. The cost of the buybacks that are turned around as stock compensation to employees is reflected in the income statement as an expense.

---

10 "Comparing NIPA Profits With S&P 500 Profits," *BEA Briefing*, March 2011.

Buybacks aren't accorded an advantage over dividends by the tax code. While buybacks may have a bullish impact on stock prices, there's certainly no guarantee that stock prices can't fall even for corporations that are buying back their shares. This discredits the notion that companies prefer buybacks because capital gains are taxed at a lower rate than dividend income. If our basic premise is correct, most companies don't view buybacks as a means of returning cash to shareholders but, rather, as offsetting all or most of the dilution caused by stock compensation. Dividends remain the way that most companies return cash to shareholders.

Deep Dive into the Data

Now let's put on our diving suits and take a deep dive into the pool of relevant data to see whether they support our analysis of buybacks:

Buybacks galore. S&P 500 buybacks totaled $4.7 trillion from the start of the bull market during the first quarter of 2009 through the final quarter of 2018, while dividends totaled $3.2 trillion (Fig. 2). Over this same period, the market capitalization of all equity issues traded in the United States soared by $27 trillion.

Dividends are the best tangible confirmation of earnings. The percentage of S&P 500 companies paying dividends rose from 73% during 2009 to 82% during 2018 (Fig. 3). In a low-interest-rate environment, they attracted lots of yield-hungry investors, driving stock prices higher.

In our narrative, buybacks have more to do with paying employees with stock grants than returning cash to shareholders. Current-dollar labor compensation totaled $76 trillion from 2011 through 2018. From this perspective, $4.3 trillion in buybacks over this same period is a relatively small sum if its main purpose is to offset dilution from stock grants.

Dividend payout ratio remains around 35%. Collectively, since the mid-1960s through the early 1990s, the S&P 500 dividend payout ratio (dividends divided by after-tax S&P 500 reported earnings) fluctuated around 50% (Fig. 4). It has tended to fluctuate around 35% since then. So historically, large corporations have tended to return cash to shareholders with a 35% to 50% dividend payout relative to after-tax profits.

The notion that buybacks have nearly doubled this measure of corporate largess to investors to close to 100% of profits makes no sense whatsoever, according to our analysis (Fig. 5). This means that the notion of the S&P 500 having a "buyback yield" comparable to the dividend yield makes no sense either (Fig. 6). In our narrative, it is a meaningless concept!

Keeping track of the share count. We acknowledge that buybacks have returned cash to shareholders and boosted earnings per share, but not by much. That's clear when we see that three measures of shares outstanding have fallen only modestly since the start of the bull market. We are mostly focusing on the data since the first quarter of 2011 through the fourth quarter of 2018 because that's the period that saw the protracted drop in the share count. During 2009, there was a big spike in share issuance by banks scrambling to raise capital following the financial crisis of 2008.

The S&P 500 divisor is used to ensure that changes in the number of shares outstanding, capital actions, and the addition or deletion of stocks to the index do not change the level of the index. It was down 7.8%, or only 1.0% per year on average, from the first quarter of 2011 through the fourth quarter of 2018 (Fig. 7). That's a small contribution to earnings-per-share growth.

The divisor is highly correlated with two alternative measures that Joe and I have concocted. For one, we divide the Fed's series on the market value of all equities traded in the United States by the S&P 500 stock price index. It was down only 12.6% (or 1.5% per year on average) from the first quarter of 2011 through the fourth quarter of 2018.

Joe also constructed a series showing the total number of basic shares outstanding for current S&P 500 companies with data for all periods and adjusted for stock splits and stock dividends (Fig. 8). Not surprisingly, his series, which starts in 2007, is highly correlated with the S&P 500 divisor. According to Joe, the share count rose 7.2% from a low of 278 billion shares during the third quarter of 2008 to a peak of 297 billion shares during the first quarter of 2011. After that, it dropped 7.7% to 275 billion shares at the end of 2018, a decline of 22 billion shares. That's an average annual decline of 1.1% since the start of 2011. That's certainly a boost to the annual growth rate of earnings per share, but a relatively small one. (See Appendix 2 for a discussion of basic versus fully diluted shares.)

Needless to say, the same conclusion follows when we compare Standard & Poor's measures of S&P 500 per-share and aggregate earnings directly (Fig. 9 and Fig. 10). From 2011 through 2018, the annual average spread between the two was only 1.3 percentage points. That certainly calls into question the credibility of the notion that the $4.3 trillion of buybacks over that period was aimed largely at boosting earnings per share.

Average price per share. Joe's share-count series allows us to calculate the average price per share of the S&P 500 companies. We do so by dividing the average market capitalization of the S&P 500 during each quarter by the number of shares outstanding at the end of each quarter (Fig. 11). The average price per share per quarter rose from a low of $25 at the end of the first quarter of 2009 to $76 at the end of 2018 (Fig. 12).

Number of shares repurchased and issued. We now easily can convert the S&P 500 buybacks data into the number of shares repurchased every quarter, simply by dividing the buybacks (in billion dollars) by the average price per share during each quarter (Fig. 13). Since the first quarter of 2011, a total of 72 billion shares were repurchased. However, over that very same period, the number of outstanding shares declined by only 22 billion!

Now we can derive gross issuance, since it is equal to buybacks less net issuance (or net buybacks when the series is negative). The result is eye-opening. Since the first quarter of 2011 through the last quarter of 2018, S&P 500 companies repurchased 72 billion shares and issued 50 billion shares, resulting in net repurchases of 22 billion shares.

Net issuance (actually, net buybacks in this case) has fluctuated at around a third of gross buybacks over this period. That explains why the amount that gross buybacks have contributed to the growth of earnings per share has been relatively small.

Buybacks driven by compensation. It's true that buybacks are driven by compensation, but not in the way that Progressive politicians believe. Buybacks do not significantly boost earnings per share to the benefit of corporations' fat-cat executives and directors or its other large, rich shareholders.

They simply reflect an accounting procedure necessary to avoid dilution when employees are paid in company shares. We can get a rough idea of how much compensation is paid via shares. To do so, we simply multiply gross issuance by the average price per share of the S&P 500 (Fig. 15).

Assuming that the value of all gross issuance of stock is for compensation (which must be somewhat of an exaggeration), this series' four-quarter sum rose from $331 billion in 2011 to $532 billion in 2018. Annualizing this series and dividing it by the compensation of all employees (including wages, salaries, bonuses, and benefits—also at an annual rate) suggests that stock compensation accounted for an average of only 4% of total employee compensation over the years from 2011 through 2018 (Fig. 16).

The Fed's Accounts

All of the above brings me back full circle to *The New York Times* article linked above, which cited Goldman Sachs data showing that only corporations are buying equities. Actually, the data come from the Fed, and they show that nonfinancial corporations (NFCs) have been huge buyers of stocks for the past 15 years, as retirements (i.e., resulting from buybacks and M&A activity) well exceed gross issuance (including initial public offerings, seasoned equity offerings, and private equity). Not surprisingly, the Fed's series for net NFC equity issuance is highly correlated with the S&P 500 buybacks series, which the Fed uses to compile its series (Fig. 17, Fig. 18, Fig. 19, Fig. 20, and Fig. 21).

Strangely, the Fed's data don't cover employee stock plans. The Fed's website includes a note titled "Equity Issuance and Retirement by Nonfinancial Corporations."[11] It carefully explains how the data series on equity issuance is constructed. It states:

> The figure also indicates that equity retirements have been consistently greater than issuances over this period, resulting in the negative values for net equity issuance reported in the Financial Accounts of the United States. This reflects the

11 "Equity Issuance and Retirement by Nonfinancial Corporations," *FEDS Notes*, June 16, 2017.

> continued importance of share repurchases as a
> means of distributing earnings to shareholders,
> due in part to the tax advantage to shareholders
> of repurchases when compared to dividend pay-
> outs. … In addition, firms also use repurchases to
> offset the dilution of existing shareholders that
> occurs through the granting of equity to employ-
> ees and executives, a common incentive compen-
> sation device.

I disagree with all but the first and last sentences of this statement for reasons discussed above.

The Fed compiles quarterly data on the flow of funds in the *Financial Accounts of the United States*. Table F.223 tracks the supply and demand for corporate equities.[12] It shows net repurchases of $168 billion during 2018, which includes net issuance of $311 billion in shares of exchange-traded funds and $128 billion of stock issued by foreign corporations.

Excluding both of those shows net repurchases of $606 billion by U.S. corporations. Using Joe's data, we get net repurchases of $275 billion. We reached out to the Fed's staff about the possibility that their equity issuance measures are not appropriately accounting for stock issuance to employees by public corporations.

---

12 *Financial Accounts of the United States*, Board of Governors of the Financial Reserve System, December 7, 2017, Table F.223.

They acknowledged that we might be right and are working to correct the problem!

Corporate Finance Nonsense

Supporting the thesis of Senator Baldwin's 33-page report, discussed above, are plenty of charts and footnotes. Not supporting it is an accurate understanding of the role of buybacks in corporate finance. On page 23 of the Baldwin report, you'll find a chart showing the strong correlation between the S&P 500 and the sum of S&P 500 buybacks and dividends. I've been using this chart to support my bullish stance almost since the start of the bull market (Fig. 22). In fact, Joe provided the data to the senator's staff for her report! Needless to say, the report manages to put a negative spin on our bullish chart as follows:

> The chart below shows buyback activity peaking and dipping in unison with the S&P 500 market index. By definition, if executives are buying high and selling low, they are managing their company's cash poorly, which should disturb all of their stakeholders—not just shareholders, but bondholders, employees, and taxpayers—as the potential for insolvency rises.

With the benefit of hindsight and additional research, Joe and I are amending our interpretation of this chart. The bull market in stocks has been driven by solid earnings delivered by a global economy that continues to grow. The coincident relationship between the S&P 500 and buybacks reflects that compensation—with some percentage paid in stock—rises in a growing economy. If compensation rises, buybacks tend to. If the economy grows, bull markets thrive. So economic growth drives both buybacks and the stock market. That's why they move in sync. It's not that buybacks drive the stock market, as widely believed.

Apparently, the authors of the Baldwin study are convinced that corporate executives are dummies and need the government's help to manage the cash of their corporations.

The intellectual godfather of this rubbish is Professor William Lazonick. As noted above, he authored a very influential article in the September 2014 *Harvard Business Review* titled "Profits Without Prosperity."[13] It is footnoted in the Baldwin report, and he is quoted several times in the report as well as by other Progressives who want to put a lid on buybacks. The professor called for "an end to open-market buybacks."

---

13 "Profits Without Prosperity," *Harvard Business Review*, September 2014.

In Lazonick's opinion, trillions of dollars have been spent to artificially boost earnings per share by lowering the share count. The money should have been used to invest in the capital and labor of corporations to make them more productive. He seems to be under the impression that buybacks and dividends have been absorbing nearly 100% of earnings, leaving nothing for capital spending.

That seems to be arithmetically correct (Fig. 23). But it is simply wrong. The problem is the claim's underlying assumption that the biggest source of corporate cash flow is profits; rather, it is depreciation allowances. This is the corporate income that is sheltered from taxation to reflect the expenses incurred in replacing depreciating assets. It's this cash that nonfinancial corporations mostly use for gross capital spending—which rose to a new record high during the third quarter of 2018 and has continued to rise in record-high territory as of this writing (Fig. 24). Recent net capital spending by NFCs is comparable to levels in previous business-cycle expansions, though making such comparisons may understate the technological enhancements in current spending (Fig. 25).

To repeat, buybacks that are offsetting stock compensation aren't financed with cash flow. The source of funds is the labor compensation item in corporate income statements, to the extent that they are related to such outlays. As we've demonstrated in this *Topical Study,* they have been used to a great extent for this purpose.

Rewarding Workers

Banning stock buybacks would be a totally unnecessary intrusion of the government in corporate finance. The real issue for Progressives isn't buybacks but compensation. They have no basis in fact by which to prove their assertion that stock compensation plans are limited to the top brass who benefit much more than their employees or even at the expense of their employees.

On the contrary, according to a post on the website of the National Center for Employee Ownership:[14]

> Data from the 2014 General Social Survey show that 22.9 million American workers own stock in their company through a 401(k) plan, ESOP, direct stock grant, or similar plan, while 8.5 million hold stock options (some employees have options and own stock through other plans, so these numbers are not additive). That means that 19.5% of the total workforce, but 34.9% of those who work for

14 "Data Show Widespread Employee Ownership in U.S.," National Center for Employee Ownership website, www.nceo.org.

companies that have stock, own stock through
some kind of benefit plan, while 7.2% of the work-
force, but 13.1% of those in companies with stock,
hold options.

Besides, the entire "problem" was manufactured by
Progressives in 1993 when they passed a law that limited the tax deductibility as a business expense of any
executive's pay above $1 million in cash, creating incen-
tives for corporations to pay highly paid employees in
stock. President Trump's Tax Cuts and Jobs Act (TCJA),
passed in December 2017, once again changed the rules
in ways likely to alter the structure of executive compensation—this time reducing stock buybacks.

Our take is that the new rules may mean fewer
stock option awards in the future, which could also
mean that fewer share repurchases will be needed to
offset their dilutive effect. No further government med-
dling is required.

Now let's consider the plight of all those workers
whom Senators Baldwin, Sanders, and Schumer want
to help:

Record employment and quits. Granted, it took
longer than usual for payroll employment to recov-
er from the previous recession, which was among the
worst since World War II. However, by May 2014, payroll employment did regain what was lost during the

severe downturn. It too has continued to move higher, and hit 151.1 million during April 2019, surpassing the previous cyclical peak during January 2008 by 9.2%. The unemployment rate has been running below 4.0% since March 2018. Job openings are at a record high, exceeding the number of people unemployed since then. The quit rate is around record highs, as workers have lots of alternative prospects for boosting their pay and their benefits.

Record income and consumption per household. Perhaps one of the biggest myths of all about our economy is that real incomes have stagnated for most Americans over the past 15-20 years. Even Donald Trump often made this claim when he was running for president. This assertion is based on one widely followed and extremely flawed inflation-adjusted measure of median household income produced annually by the Census Bureau (Fig. 26). It is based on survey data, focuses just on money income, and is pre-tax.

From the first quarter of 2000 through the fourth quarter of 2017, real GDP per household rose 19.7%. Yet over this same period, the aforementioned income series, which is available only on an annual basis, rose just 2.2%. That's stagnation for sure, and implies significantly worsening inequality. However, numerous other inflation-adjusted measures of household income and wages are broader in scope, including nonmonetary government support programs like Medicaid, food stamps, and tax credits. They are up much more over the same period.

For example, real personal income per household rose 27.0% before taxes and 29.9% after taxes over those 18 years. Skeptics will pounce on the fact that these are means, not medians, and so might be upwardly biased by the enormous incomes of the ultra-rich. I doubt that, as evidenced by real personal consumption per household, up 28.1%. The rich don't eat much more than the rest of us. My basic assumption is that there aren't enough ultra-rich—often dubbed the "1%" for a reason—to bias the mean series I've constructed for personal income and consumption.[15]

Record real wages and compensation. There can be no disputing the fact that real wages haven't been stagnating at all, notwithstanding the assertions of the three senators who want to help workers. From the start of 2000 through the end of 2017, real average hourly earnings rose 17.3% (Fig. 27). I am using the series that applies only to production and nonsupervisory workers, who tend to be rich only if they've won the lottery. They account for roughly 80% of all workers.

---

15 IRS data for tax-year 2016 show 150.3 million taxpayers filed personal tax returns. Only 1.3 million of them (i.e., 1%) had adjusted gross income exceeding $500,000.

There's more: Total real compensation—which includes wages, salaries, and benefits, per worker (using the household measure of employment)—rose 19.5% from the start of 2000 through the end of 2017, and was at a record high last year, as were all the other measures mentioned above (Fig. 28).

American households are enjoying record standards of living. Income stagnation is a myth. Income inequality isn't a myth but an inherent characteristic of free-market capitalism, an economic system that awards the biggest prizes to those entrepreneurs who benefit the most consumers with their goods and services. Perversely, inequality tends to be greatest during periods of widespread prosperity. Rather than bemoaning that development, we should celebrate that so many households are prospering, even if a few are doing so more than the rest of us.

America's free-market capitalism continues to boost the prosperity of most Americans, in my opinion, without more help from the government.

The Crony Problem

Progressives like Senators Baldwin, Sanders, and Schumer want to reduce corporate cronyism. I wholeheartedly agree with them on that, and I have some ideas on how to do so, including limiting the number of boards on which an individual may serve and compiling a "crony scoreboard" to keep track. Corporate cronyism may become a bigger problem, in my opinion, because shareholders are losing their influence over corporate managers and boards as a result of the outflows from equity mutual funds into equity exchange-traded funds. Active managers exert more shareholder influence over corporate governance issues than do passively managed funds.

SEC Commissioner Robert J. Jackson, Jr., who was appointed by President Donald Trump, also has some good ideas on how to regulate some games played by corporate executives with buybacks. In a June 11, 2018 speech, he discussed "how to give corporate managers incentives to create sustainable long-term value."[16] When he joined the SEC in early 2018, he asked his staff to study 385 buybacks over the previous 15 months. Jackson was shocked to learn:

---

16 Robert J. Jackson, Jr., "Stock Buybacks and Corporate Cashouts," June 11, 2018 speech.

> In half of the buybacks we studied, at least one
> executive sold shares in the month following the
> buyback announcement. In fact, twice as many
> companies have insiders selling in the eight days
> after a buyback announcement as sell on an ordi-
> nary day. So right after the company tells the mar-
> ket that the stock is cheap, executives overwhelm-
> ingly decide to sell.

To fix this problem, Jackson favors adopting an SEC rule that would "encourage executives to keep their skin in the game for the long term." In his opinion, safe harbor should be denied to companies that choose to allow executives to cash out during a buyback.

There is certainly room for improvement in corporate governance. On the other hand, I see no need for limiting or banning buybacks. Most corporate managers have ample incentive to make their companies as successful as possible irrespective of buybacks, as evidenced by record earnings both on a per-share basis and in aggregate.

Technology and the Other Sectors

Our analysis of the role of share repurchases in the corporate financial activities of the S&P 500 suggests that

Progressives are misguided in their obsession with limiting or even banning buybacks. That's not as clear cut when the spotlight is on the S&P 500 Information Technology sector.

This was the focus of an April 14, 2019 Bloomberg article titled "Big Tech's Big Tax Ruse: Industry Splurges on Buybacks."[17] The two authors berate the tech giants for pushing for Trump's tax cuts with promises to expand their capacity and payrolls.

The authors find little evidence that Big Tech kept its end of the bargain in 2018. Instead, they observe that these companies spent most of their tax windfalls on buybacks:

> The top 10 U.S. tech companies spent more than $169 billion purchasing their shares in 2018, a 55 percent jump from the year before the tax changes, according to data compiled by Bloomberg. The industry as a whole authorized the greatest number of share buybacks ever recorded, totaling $387 billion, according to TrimTabs Investment Research. That's more than triple the amount in 2017.

I asked Joe to run our analysis of S&P 500 buybacks just for the S&P 500 Information Technology sector. Here are his major findings:

---

17 "Big Tech's Big Tax Ruse: Industry Splurges on Buybacks," Bloomberg, April 14, 2019.

From the first quarter of 2011 through the fourth quarter of 2018, the share count for the current tech companies in the S&P 500 has dropped 17.3%, or 2.2% per year on average, according to Joe's calculations (Fig. 29). (The sector's S&P divisor plunged during third-quarter 2018 as a result of the shifting of companies into the Communication Services and Consumer Discretionary sectors.)

Our data show that 2018 was an outlier: The share-count declines during previous years didn't add much to earnings per share. During 2018, the decline boosted the sector's earnings per share by 14 percentage points (Fig. 30).

The "wrinkle" in our analysis of buybacks is that we can derive the average price per share of the stocks in the S&P 500 Tech sector by dividing the sector's market capitalization by Joe's share-count series for the sector (Fig. 31). That allows us to convert the sector's buybacks in dollars to the actual number of shares that have been repurchased (Fig. 32).

The question is what percentage of these gross buybacks are actually used to reduce the share count, as opposed to offsetting the impact of employee stock compensation plans and M&A activity? The answer is that it has been a volatile data series, fluctuating around 50% since 2011, which is above the roughly 33% figure we previously derived for the overall S&P 500 (Fig. 33 and Fig. 34).

Finally, here are the percentage changes in the share counts of the 11 sectors of the S&P 500 from the first quarter of 2011 through the fourth quarter of 2018: Real Estate (38.6%), Utilities (20.3), Materials (10.8), Communication Services (6.6), Energy (0.4), S&P 500 (-7.7), Health Care (-9.4), Financials (-10.3), Consumer Staples (-10.7), Consumer Discretionary (-12.2), Industrials (-13.6), and Information Technology (-17.3).

Negligible Impact

Warren Buffett is a big fan of buybacks. In his latest letter to the shareholders of Berkshire Hathaway, Buffett wrote:

> All of our major holdings enjoy excellent economics, and most use a portion of their retained earnings to repurchase their shares. We very much like that: If Charlie [Munger] and I think an investee's stock is underpriced, we rejoice when management employs some of its earnings to increase Berkshire's ownership percentage. Here's one example drawn from the table above: Berkshire's holdings of American Express have remained unchanged over the past eight

years. Meanwhile, our ownership increased from 12.6% to 17.9% because of repurchases made by the company. Last year, Berkshire's portion of the $6.9 billion earned by American Express was $1.2 billion, about 96% of the $1.3 billion we paid for our stake in the company. When earnings increase and shares outstanding decrease, owners—over time—usually do well."[18]

I asked Joe to calculate the share count for American Express. He reports that the company's share count was reduced by an average of 1.1% *per quarter* since the first quarter of 2011 through the fourth quarter of 2018, and is down 28.9% overall during this period (Fig. 35).

He did the same analysis for each of the companies in the S&P 500. Among these companies, plenty have had aggressive buyback programs aimed not only at offsetting dilution from stock compensation but also at boosting earnings per share. However, as demonstrated in this *Topical Study,* the overall impact of buybacks on S&P 500 earnings per share has been relatively small.

Joe examined whether S&P 500 companies with reductions in their basic shares outstanding since the first quarter of 2011 had outperformed the index over the eight-year period. He didn't find a noticeable perfor-mance difference between companies that had increased

18 February 23, 2019 letter to Berkshire Hathaway shareholders from Chairman of the Board Warren E. Buffett.

and those that had decreased their share counts. But among those companies that had share-count reductions, there was slight outperformance correlating with how much a company's share count was reduced. Here is a summary of his findings, based on share-count data shown in our report, *S&P 500 Basic Share Count, Q1-2011 to Q1-2019.*[19]

Joe looked at 458 of the 505 issues in the S&P 500 with price performance data through their calendar first quarter of 2019.[20] The 47 issues not included in his study went public after the first quarter of 2011.

Joe found that the stock prices of all companies rose an average of 165%. The 175 issues with increased share counts had a slightly higher gain of 170%, while the 281 issues with decreased share counts rose a slightly lower 163%. (Two companies' share counts were unchanged.)

That was a little surprising, but not unexpected. Joe surmises that companies with higher share counts after the past eight years issued additional shares primarily to finance M&A activity. These companies' shares outperformed because the M&A activity presented

---

19 *S&P 500 Basic Share Count, Q1-2011 to Q1-2019*, Yardeni Research, July 1, 2019.

20 We extended the period of analysis from the final quarter of 2018 through the first quarter of 2019 to offset the extreme selloff that occurred at the end of last year with the dramatic rebound at the beginning of this year.

them with better opportunities for cost reductions and growth of their revenues and earnings.

Looking at the companies with share-count decreases and grouping them in tranches by degree of decrease, Joe noted that their average price change improved negligibly the more shares were removed. Among the 149 companies that reduced shares by more than 15%, the average price gain was 163%, slightly worse than the all-company average of 165%. The share prices of the 100 firms with at least a 20% decrease in share count rose 174%; the share prices of the 41 companies with more than a 30% drop in share count rose by nearly the same amount, 175%; and the 16 companies with at least a 35% decrease in share count rose an average of 185% in share price.

On balance, buybacks reduced the share count of the S&P 500 by only 8.0% over the period from the first quarter of 2011 through the first quarter of 2019, or 1.0% per year.

Hence, we again conclude that the impact of buybacks on earnings per share has been greatly exaggerated. That's because we found that roughly two-thirds of buybacks may be mostly offsetting stocks issued as labor compensation. Rather than boosting earnings per share, most buybacks are aimed at reducing the share-count dilution that results from compensating employees with stock. Limiting them or banning them by law would deprive lots of employees, not just top managements, from having an equity stake by which to share in their companies' success.

Appendix 1

Excerpts from BEA Briefings
on Expensing of Stock Options

Carol E. Moylan, "Employee Stock Options and the National Economic Accounts," *BEA Briefing*, February 2008

Employee stock options provide employees with the right to purchase, within a specified time period (often 10 years), shares of their company's stock at a "strike" price set by the company. For publicly traded stock, the "strike" price (also called the grant or exercise price) is usually the market price of the stock at the time the option is granted. There is usually a minimum waiting period—referred to as the "vesting" period—during which the employee must remain employed by the company before the individual may exercise the option (that is, purchase the stock). The average vesting period is usually 3 years after the time of grant.

Employee stock options are granted as part of an overall compensation package. In some cases, employees accept lower current-period wages and salaries with the expectation that the growth in the market value of the company stock will more than offset the reduction to their wages. For other employees, stock options are an additional benefit that makes working for a particular company more attractive. From the employer's perspective, options are often seen as a way to retain employees, as the options vest over several years. Additionally, for key executives, stock options are used as an incentive tool designed to link individual pay to the company's stock performance. The exercising of stock options has become a significant component of compensation for chief executive officers (chart 1 [find chart, titled "Average Executive Pay," on page 1 of linked report]).

In the United States, two major types of employee stock options have emerged: nonqualified stock options (NSOs) and incentive stock options (ISOs). The most prevalent stock option is the NSO. NSOs are often referred to as "compensatory" options because their use gives rise to compensation expenses on a company's tax returns. When NSOs are exercised, the difference between the current market price at the time of exercise and the strike price is reported as wages on the tax returns of the employer and the employee. The employee incurs an associated tax liability, and the company receives a tax deduction for the difference between the current market price and the strike price. Despite this tax treatment, until 2005, companies were not required to record any stock option expenses on financial statements.

Andrew W. Hodge, "Comparing NIPA Profits with S&P 500 Profits," *BEA Briefing*, March 2011

The respective treatments of employee stock options differ significantly. NIPA accounting and tax accounting have always treated employee stock options as an expense only when (and if) options are exercised. It is an operating expense and therefore always a cost deduction in the NIPA profits calculation. However, GAAP accounting now expenses options at grant or on a schedule beginning at grant. The valuation of the options is based on a formula that is in turn based on the right to eventual exercise, and considerable discretion is allowed. Until 2006, GAAP option expense reporting was completely at a company's discretion and reported as a nonoperating expense or, often, not reported at all. Since 2006, options grant expense was mandated by GAAP. It was included in S&P reporting starting in 2006 as an operating profits deduction.

Source: Bureau of Economic Analysis, U.S. Department of Commerce.

Appendix 2
Basic Versus Fully Diluted Shares

Basic outstanding shares and fully diluted shares are two different methodologies for companies to report their per-share earnings. The Financial Accounting Standards Board in 1997 required companies to report both results under GAAP rules, which stipulate the following:

- The basic earnings-per-share (EPS) calculation takes the net income of common shares for a period of time and divides it by the average number of outstanding shares for the same period.

- Diluted EPS calculations include the additional shares assuming that all convertible securities of a company were all exercised. Convertible securities include convertible bonds, convertible preferred stock, stock options, rights, and warrants. Out-of-money options are not included in diluted EPS.

One of the mainstays of GAAP accounting is that financial statements should be as conservative as possible. Generally, fully diluted EPS is lower than basic EPS if the company made a profit; similarly, diluted EPS will show a lower loss than basic EPS in the situation of a loss. This is because the profits and losses must be divided among more shares.

For the S&P 500, Standard & Poor's reports earnings both ways. Yet Standard & Poor's calculations of both market capitalization and the divisor are based on the basic number of shares.

We only use the fully diluted EPS to match I/B/E/S fully diluted data. However, Joe notes that fully diluted shares are additional shares that may or may not be created in the future. They are "event-based contracts" that have not taken effect yet. By no means is fully diluted shares an ironclad number that will be achieved in the future. It's just a worse-case scenario.

That's why our analysis of buybacks in this Topical Study uses basic shares even though diluted is used for earnings reporting.

Buybacks should be compared to basic shares outstanding at any given time to reflect the repurchases of those actual shares.

Joe compared the basic versus diluted share count of the S&P 500 from the first quarter of 2011 through the fourth quarter of 2018. The former fell 7.7%, while the latter declined 8.2% (Fig. 36).

Since EPS is widely reported on a fully diluted basis, corporations have a big incentive to offset dilution resulting from stock compensation with buybacks. In other words, most buybacks are motivated by an attempt to offset the dilution of EPS rather than to boost EPS by reducing the basic share count.

Source: Yardeni Research, Inc.

Note to Readers

These Topical Studies examine issues,
which were discussed in my book,
Predicting the Markets: A Professional Autobiography (2018),
but in greater detail and on a more current basis.
Other studies in this series can be found at
www.yardenibook.com/studies.

The charts included at the end
of this study were current as of July 2019.
Updates (in color) are also available at
www.yardenibook.com/studies.

Institutional investors are welcome
to sign up for our research service on a
four-week complimentary basis at
www.yardeni.com/trial-registration.

Figure 1.

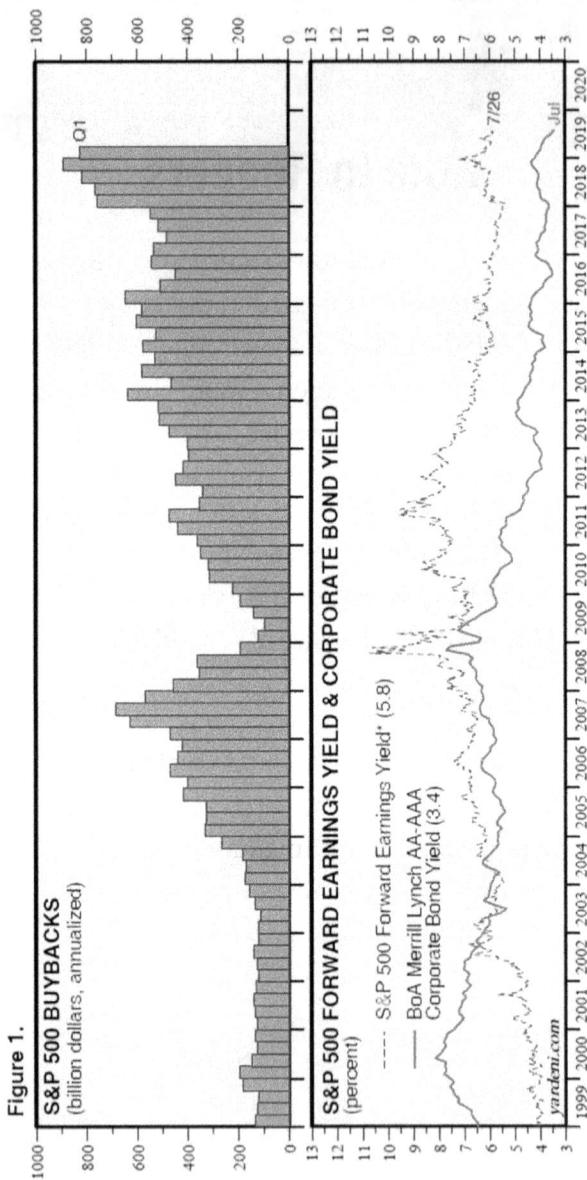

S&P 500 BUYBACKS
(billion dollars, annualized)

S&P 500 FORWARD EARNINGS YIELD & CORPORATE BOND YIELD
(percent)

---- S&P 500 Forward Earnings Yield* (5.8)

—— BoA Merrill Lynch AA-AAA
Corporate Bond Yield (3.4)

yardeni.com

* Forward earnings (time-weighted average of consensus operating earnings estimates for current and next year) divided by S&P 500 stock price index.
Source: I/B/E/S data by Refinitiv. Standard & Poor's and Bank of America Merrill Lynch

Figure 2.

S&P 500 DIVIDENDS & BUYBACKS
(trillion dollars, annualized)

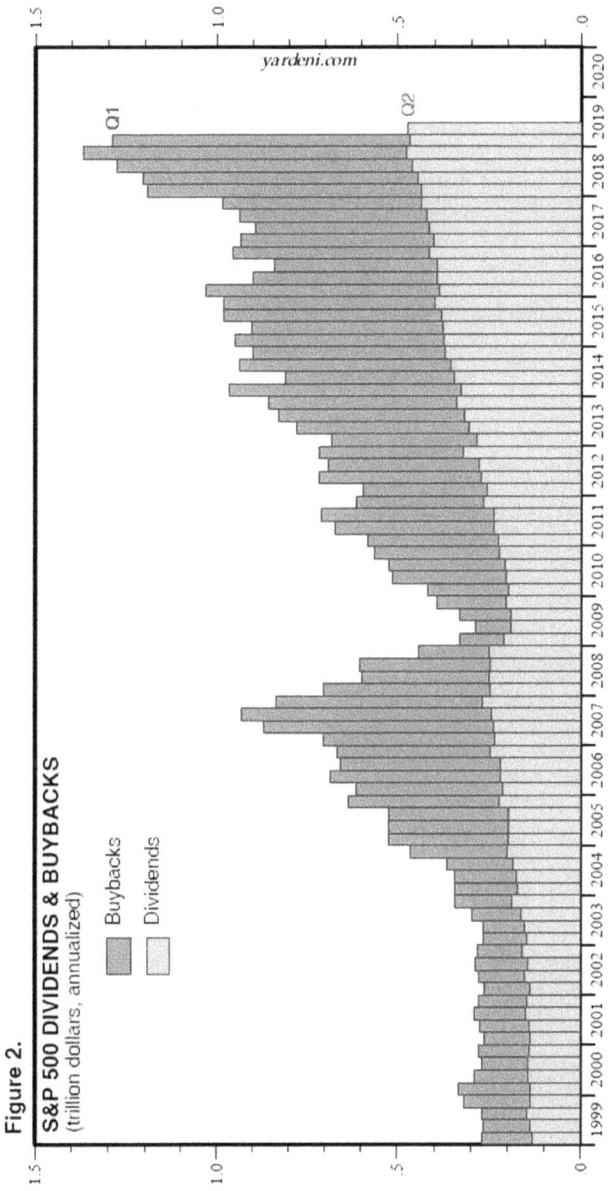

Source: Standard & Poor's.

Figure 3.

S&P 500 COMPANIES PAYING A DIVIDEND
(percent of total)

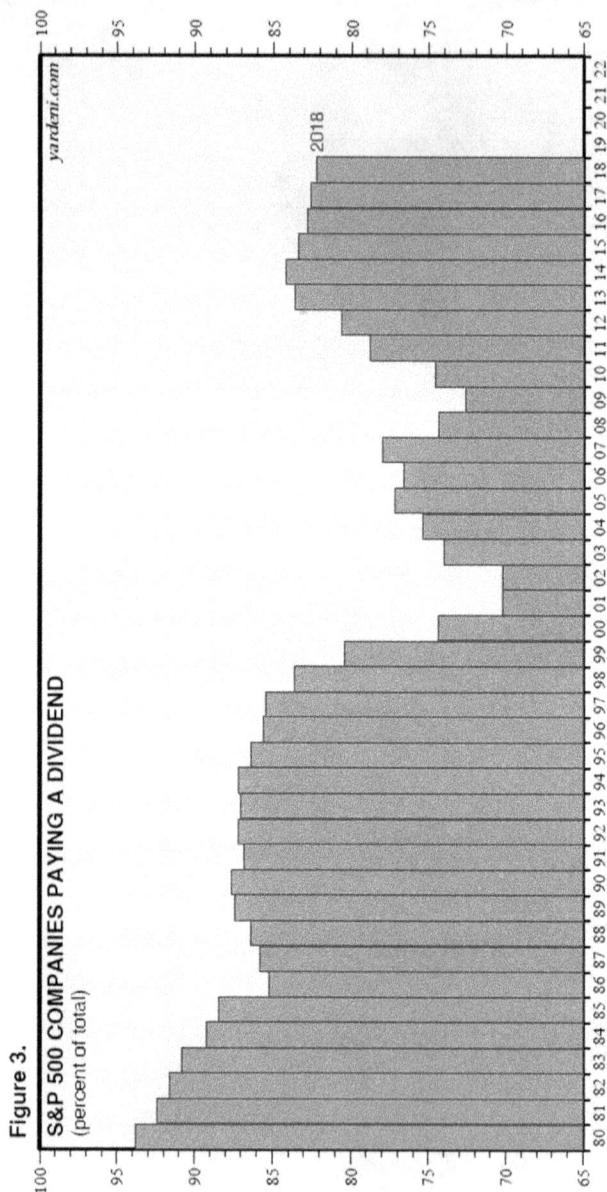

Source: Standard & Poor's.

Figure 4.

DIVIDEND PAYOUT RATIOS
(percent)

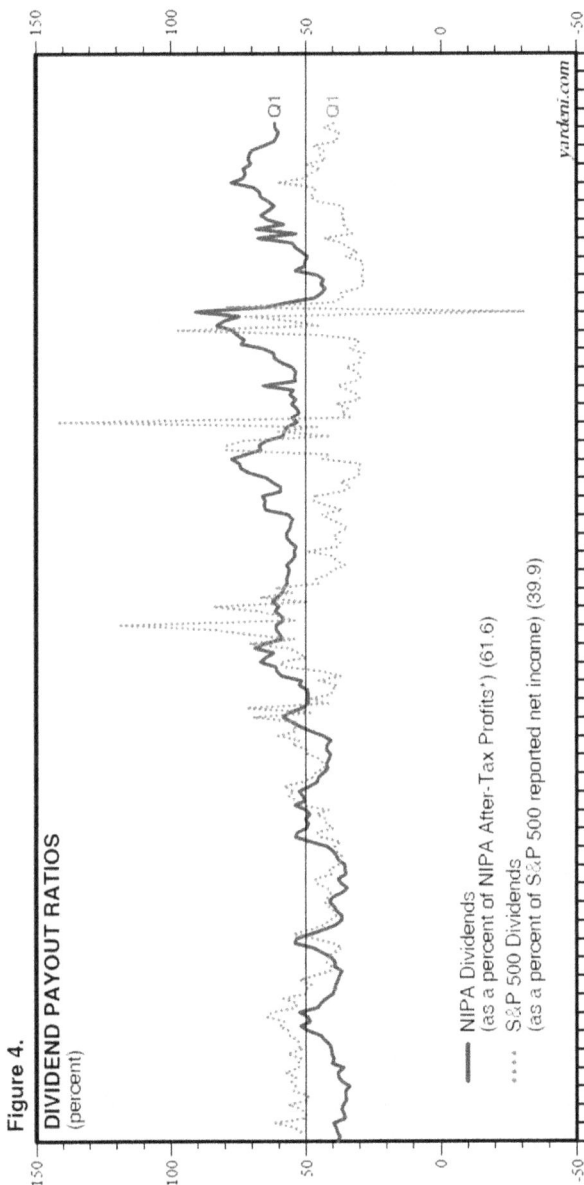

—— NIPA Dividends
(as a percent of NIPA After-Tax Profits*) (61.6)

···· S&P 500 Dividends
(as a percent of S&P 500 reported net income) (39.9)

yardeni.com

* From Current Production Including IVA & CCadj. These two adjustments restate the historical cost basis used in profits tax accounting for inventory withdrawals and depreciation to the current cost measures used in GDP.
Source: Federal Reserve Board. Financial Accounts of the United States. Standard & Poor's and Bureau of Economic Analysis

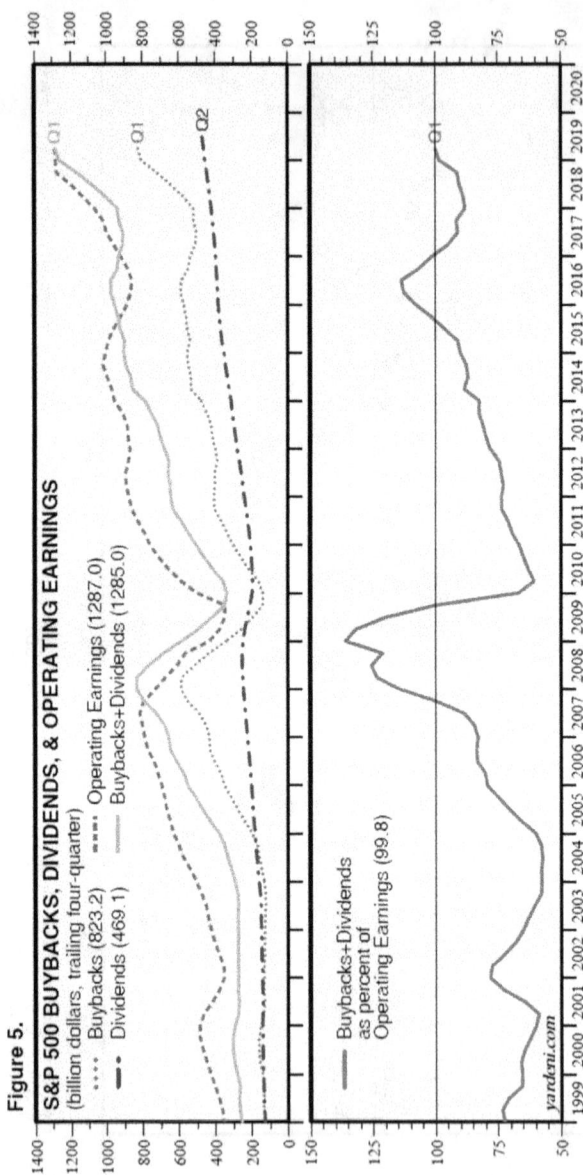

Figure 5.

S&P 500 BUYBACKS, DIVIDENDS, & OPERATING EARNINGS
(billion dollars, trailing four-quarter)

- ····· Buybacks (823.2)
- ▬▬▬ Operating Earnings (1287.0)
- –·–·– Dividends (469.1)
- ▬▬▬ Buybacks+Dividends (1285.0)

Buybacks+Dividends
as percent of
Operating Earnings (99.8)

yardeni.com

Source: Standard & Poor's.

Figure 6.

S&P 500 DIVIDEND & BUYBACK YIELDS
(percent using four-quarter sums)

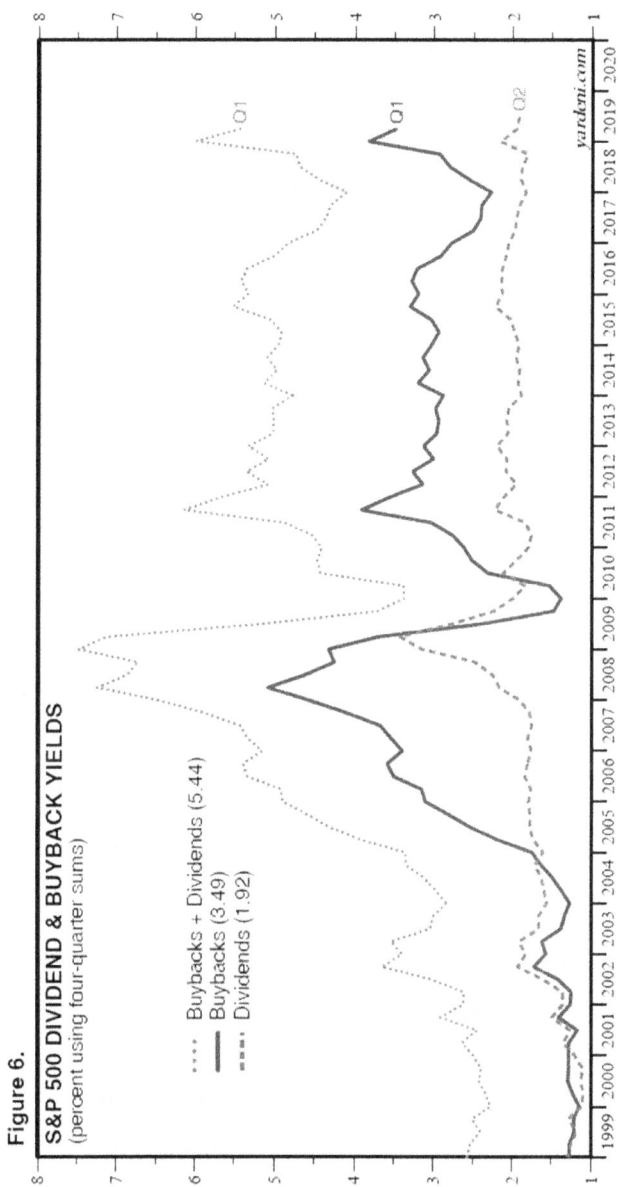

···· Buybacks + Dividends (5.44)
— Buybacks (3.49)
- - - Dividends (1.92)

yardeni.com

Source: Standard & Poor's

Figure 7.

PROXIES OF US EQUITIES SHARE COUNT

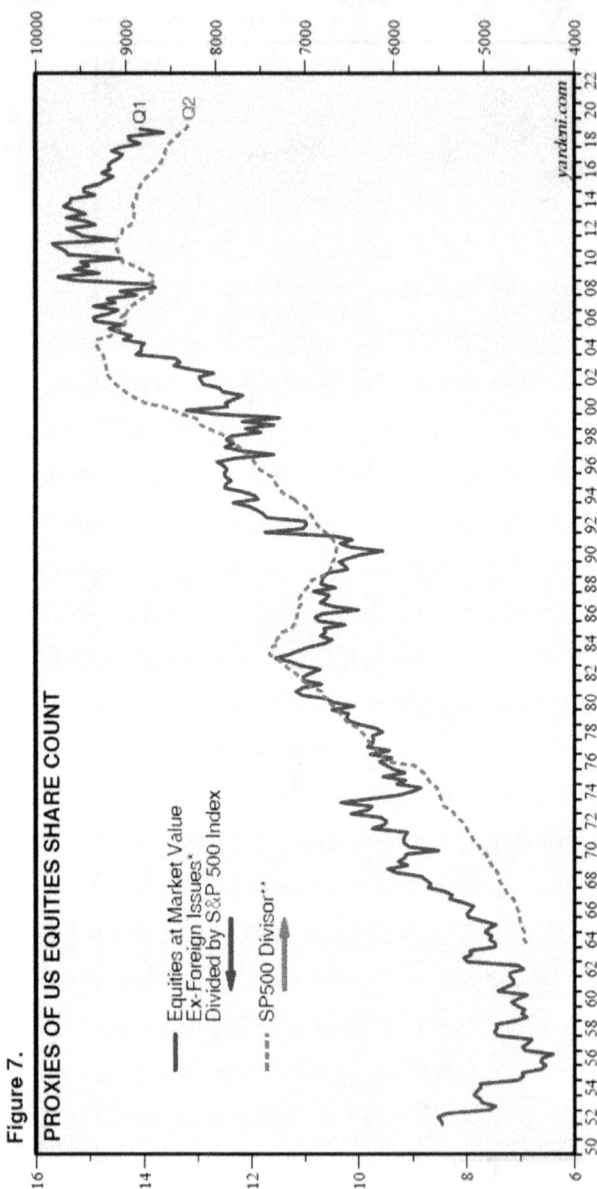

—— Equities at Market Value
Ex-Foreign Issues*
Divided by S&P 500 Index

- - - SP500 Divisor**

yardeni.com

* Excludes holdings by US residents of foreign corporate equities, investment fund shares, and ADRs.
** Divisor is used to ensure that changes in shares outstanding, capital actions, and the addition or deletion of stocks to the index do not change the level
of the index.
Source: Federal Reserve Board and Standard & Poor's.

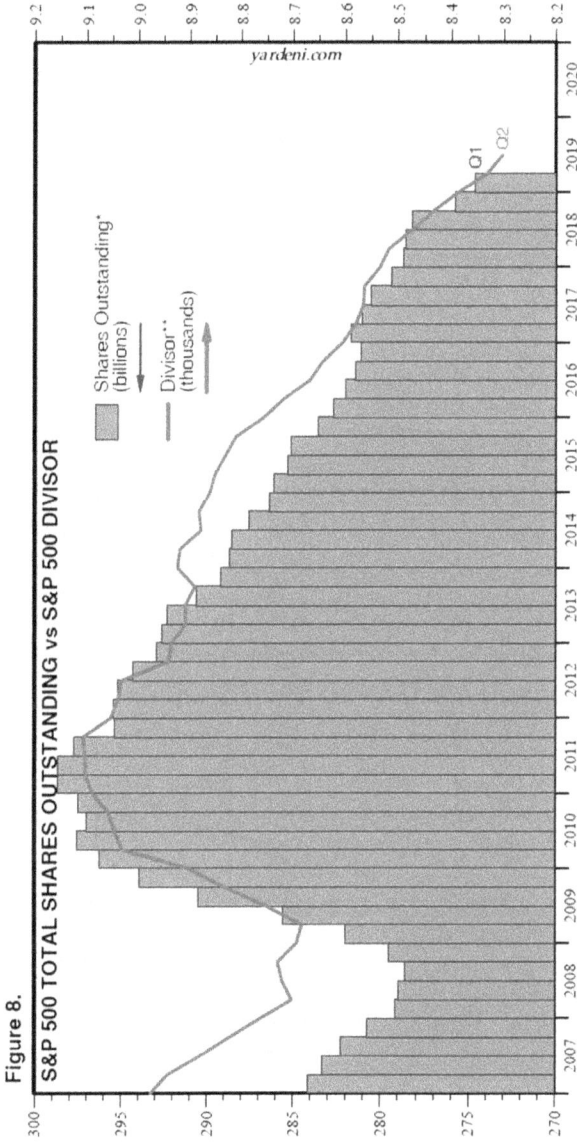

Figure 8.
S&P 500 TOTAL SHARES OUTSTANDING vs S&P 500 DIVISOR

* Total basic shares outstanding (billions) for current S&P 500 companies with data for all periods and adjusted for stock splits and stock dividends.
** Divisor is used to ensure that changes in shares outstanding, capital actions, and the addition or deletion of stocks to the index do not change the level of the index.
Source: Yardeni Research, I/B/E/S data by Refinitiv, and Standard & Poor's

Figure 9.

S&P 500 AGGREGATE OPERATING INCOME vs
S&P 500 OPERATING INCOME PER SHARE
(yearly percent change in 4-quarter average)

S&P 500 Operating Income
—— Aggregate* (13.9)
···· Per Share (17.0)

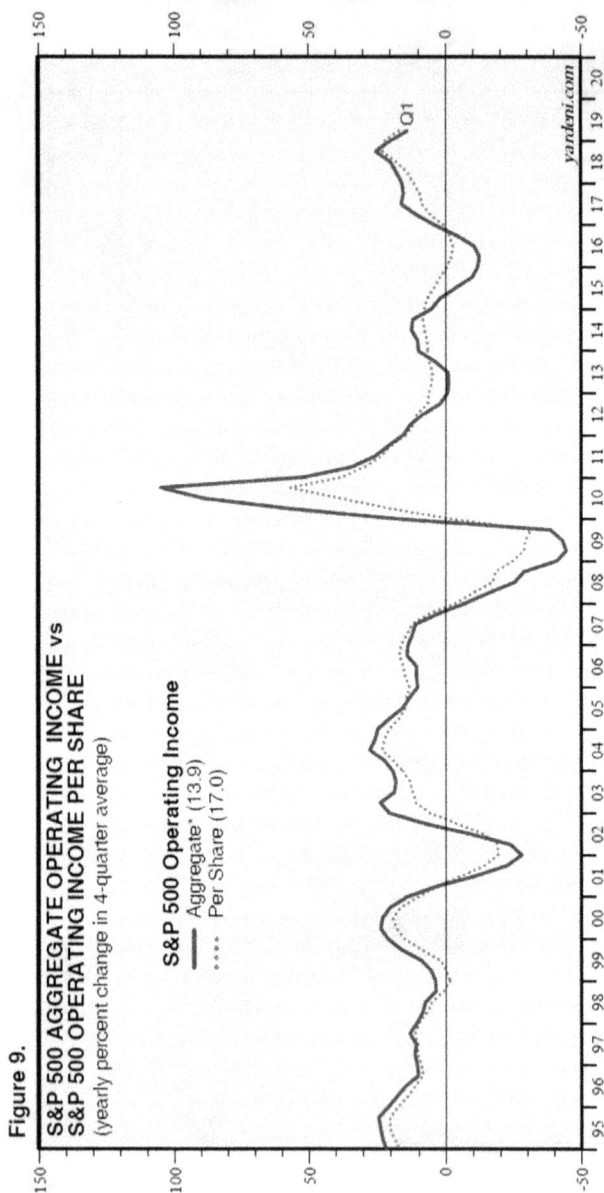

yardeni.com

95 | 96 | 97 | 98 | 99 | 00 | 01 | 02 | 03 | 04 | 05 | 06 | 07 | 08 | 09 | 10 | 11 | 12 | 13 | 14 | 15 | 16 | 17 | 18 | 19 | 20

* Aggregate earnings is derived by multiplying S&P 500 earnings per share by the S&P 500 divisor for each quarter.
Source: I/B/E/S data by Refinitiv and Standard & Poor's.

Figure 10.

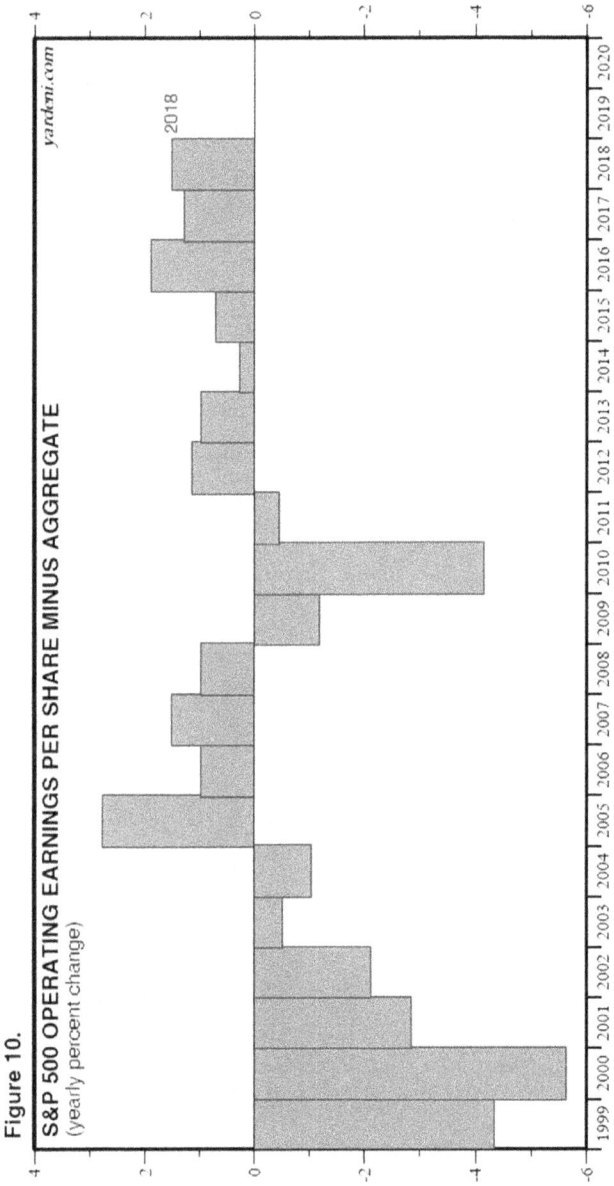

S&P 500 OPERATING EARNINGS PER SHARE MINUS AGGREGATE
(yearly percent change)

Source: I B E'S data by Refinitiv and Standard & Poor's.

Figure 11.

S&P 500 MARKET CAPITALIZATION*
(trillion dollars)

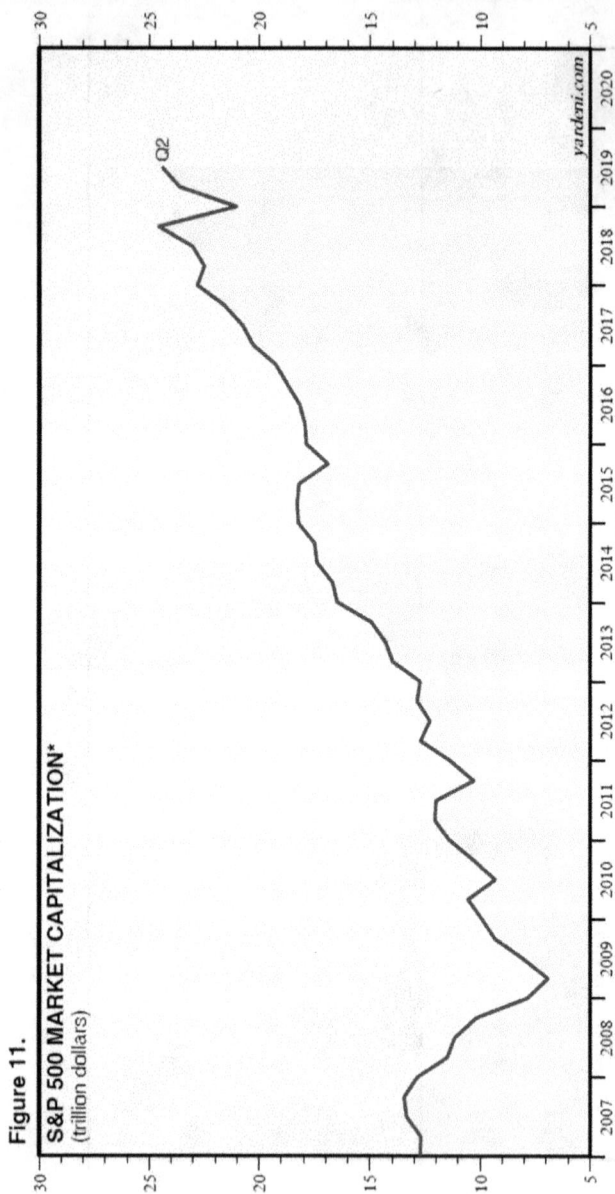

* Data shown are daily averages for each quarter.
Source: Standard & Poor's and Haver Analytics.

Figure 12.

S&P 500 IMPLIED AVERAGE PRICE PER SHARE*
(dollars)

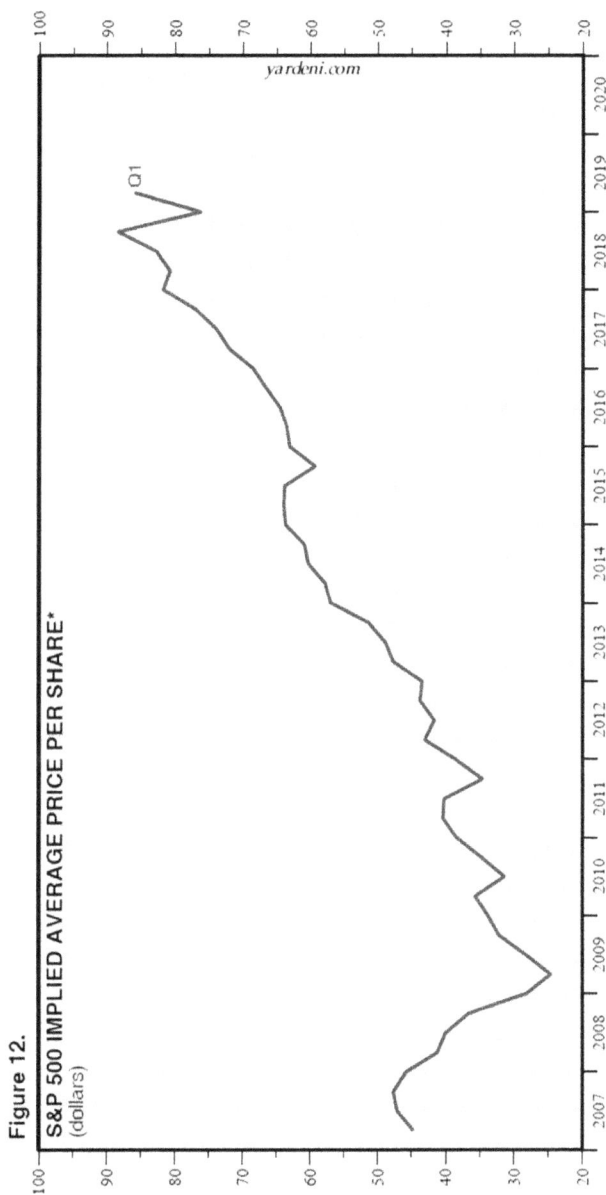

* Derived using daily averages for each quarter of market capitalization for S&P 500 divided by basic shares outstanding for all S&P 500
   companies at the end of each quarter.
   Source: Yardeni Research and I/B/E/S data by Refinitiv.

Figure 13.

S&P 500 SHARES ISSUANCE AND BUYBACKS (billion shares)

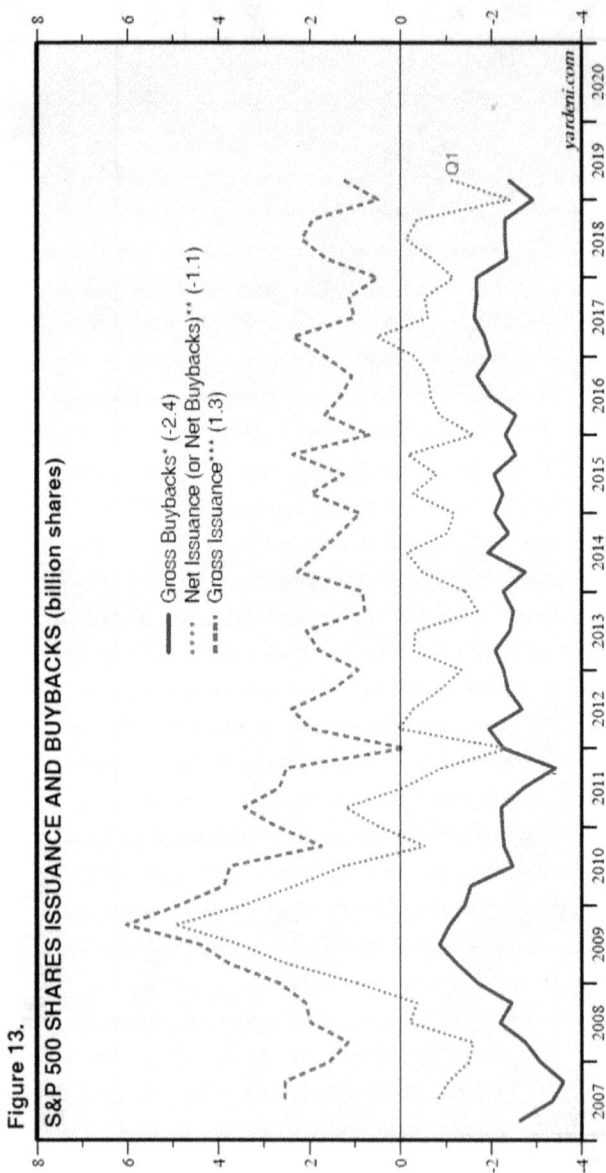

—— Gross Buybacks* (-2.4)
········· Net Issuance (or Net Buybacks)** (-1.1)
------ Gross Issuance*** (1.3)

yardeni.com

* Series compiled using S&P's total buybacks and YRI's basic shares outstanding for all S&P 500 companies at the end of each quarter.
** Series derived by YRI using quarterly changes in basic shares outstanding for all S&P 500 companies at the end of each quarter.
*** Series derived by YRI as Net Issuance + Gross Buybacks.
Source: Yardeni Research and I/B/E/S data by Refinitiv.

Figure 14.

S&P 500 NET BUYBACKS* AS PERCENT OF GROSS BUYBACKS**
(using 4-quarter sums)

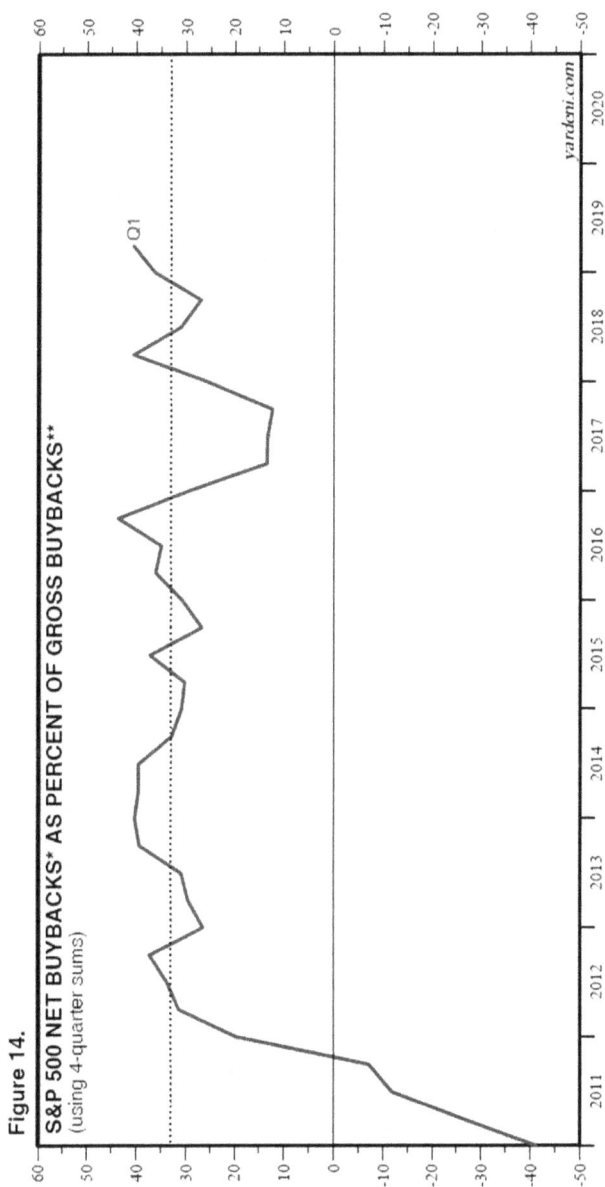

* Series derived by YRI using quarterly changes in basic shares outstanding for all S&P 500 companies at the end of each quarter.
** Series compiled by S&P.
Source: Yardeni Research and I/B/E/S data by Refinitiv.

Figure 15.

S&P 500 SHARES ISSUANCE AND BUYBACKS
(billion dollars, derived using average S&P 500 price per share)
(quarterly flows)

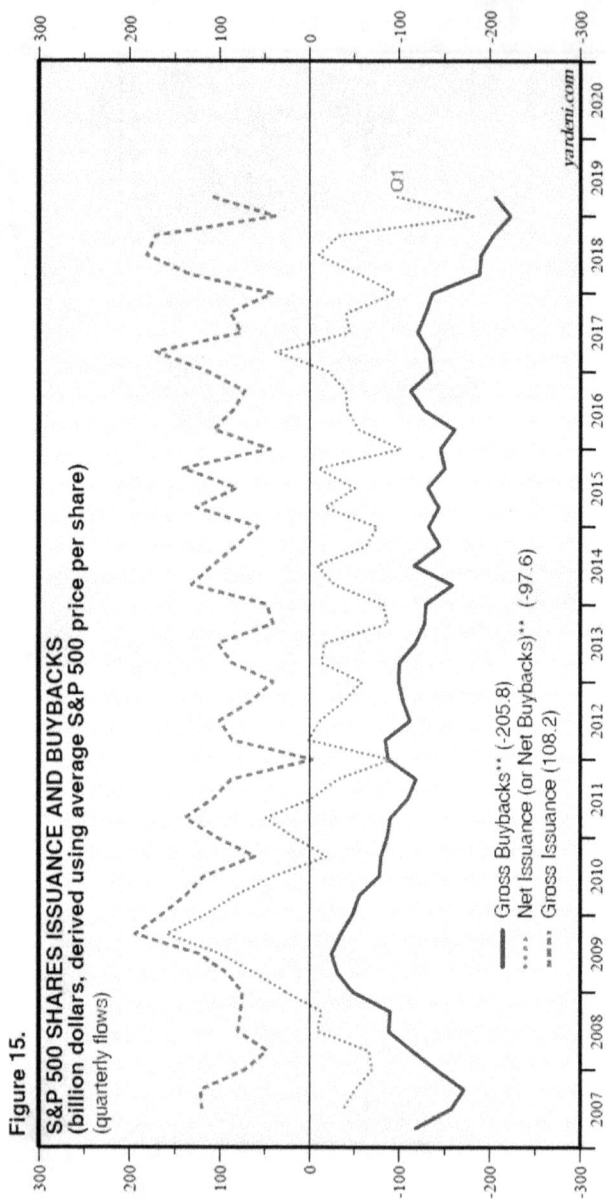

—— Gross Buybacks** (-205.8)
···· Net Issuance (or Net Buybacks)** (-97.6)
---- Gross Issuance (108.2)

yardeni.com

* Series compiled using S&P's total buybacks and YRI's basic shares outstanding for all S&P 500 companies at the end of each quarter.
** Series derived by YRI using quarterly changes in basic shares outstanding for all S&P 500 companies at the end of each quarter.
*** Series derived by YRI as Net Issuance + Gross Buybacks.
Source: Yardeni Research and I/B/E/S data by Refinitiv.

Figure 16.

VALUE OF GROSS ISSUANCE OF SHARES BY S&P 500 COMPANIES
(as a percent of compensation of all employees)

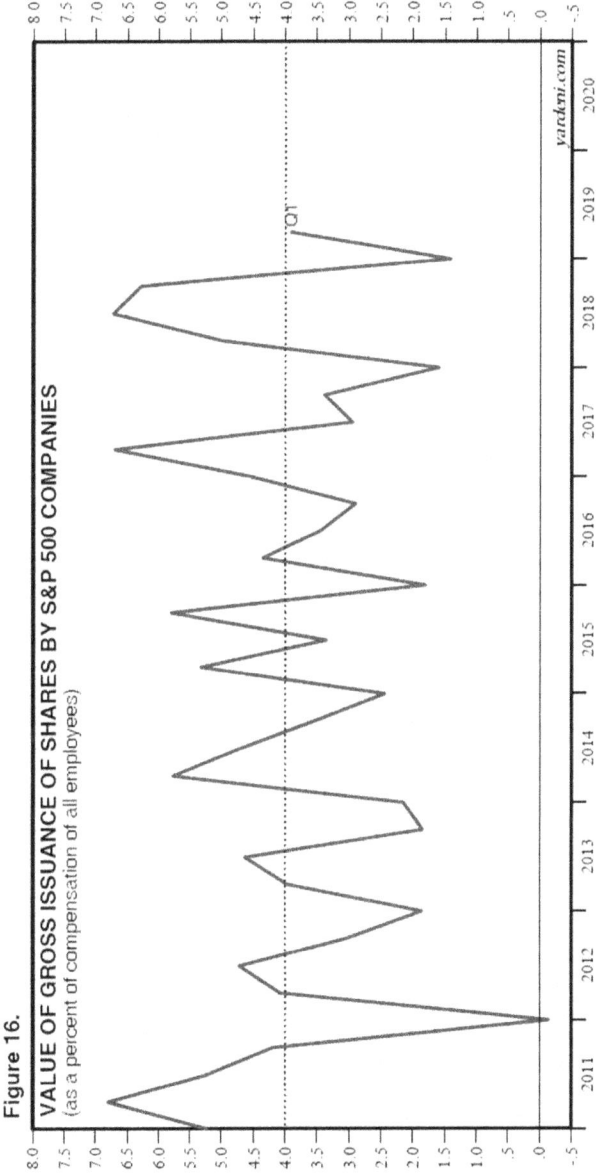

Source: Bureau of Labor Statistics and Federal Reserve Board Financial Accounts of the United States

yardeni.com

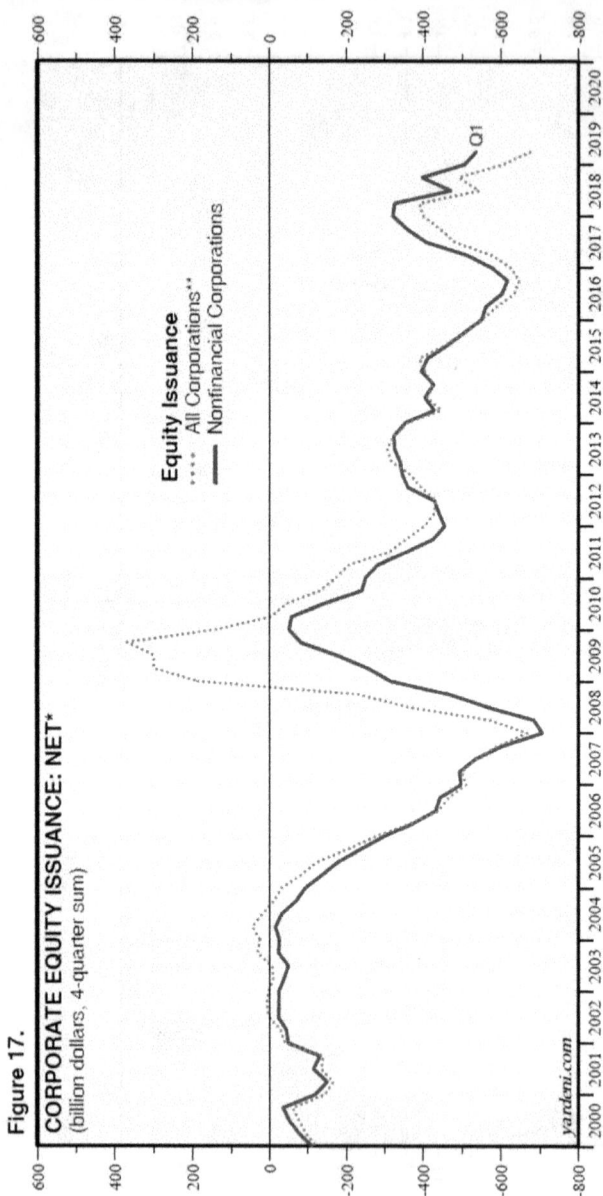

Figure 17.

CORPORATE EQUITY ISSUANCE: NET*
(billion dollars, 4-quarter sum)

Equity Issuance
•••• All Corporations**
—— Nonfinancial Corporations

Q1

yardeni.com

* Gross issuance (including initial public offerings, seasoned equity offerings, and private equity) minus retirements (including buybacks and M&A activity).
Does not include employee stock plans.
** Net issues excluding exchange-traded funds and rest of the world.
Source: Federal Reserve Board, Financial Accounts of the United States.

Figure 18.

NONFINANCIAL CORPORATE EQUITY ISSUANCE: GROSS
(billion dollars, 4-quarter sum)

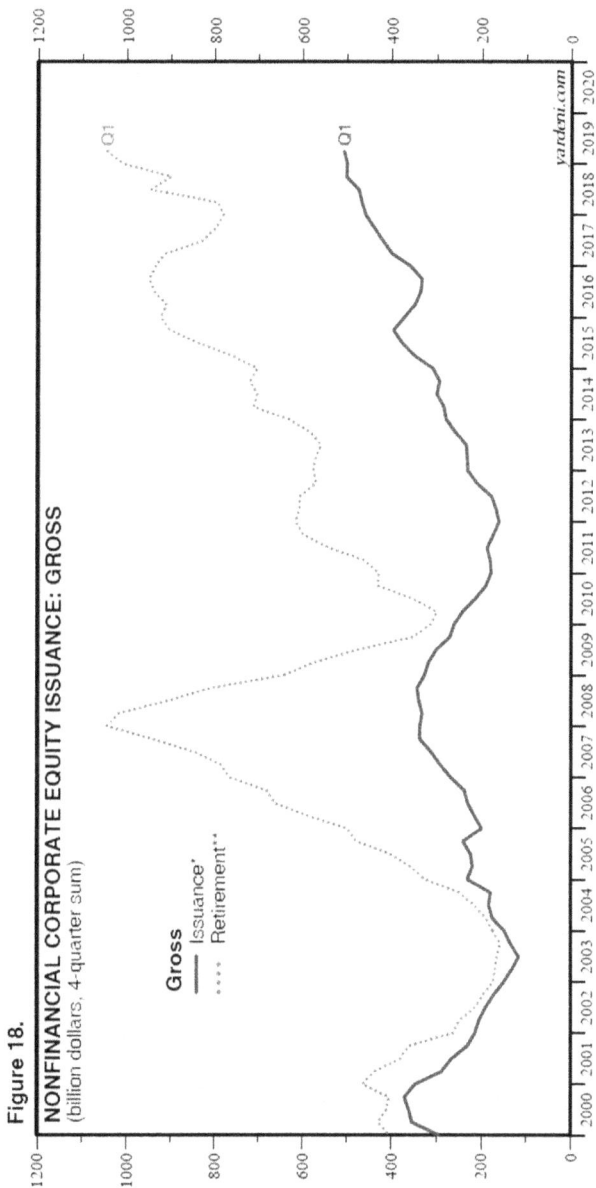

Gross
— Issuance*
···· Retirement**

* Issuance includes initial public offerings, seasoned equity offerings, and private equity. Retirements includes buybacks and M&A activity. Does not include employee stock plans.
** Repurchases plus M&A
Source: Federal Reserve Board Financial Accounts of the United States.

yardeni.com

Figure 19.

NONFINANCIAL CORPORATE EQUITY ISSUANCE: RETIREMENTS
(billion dollars, 4-quarter sum)

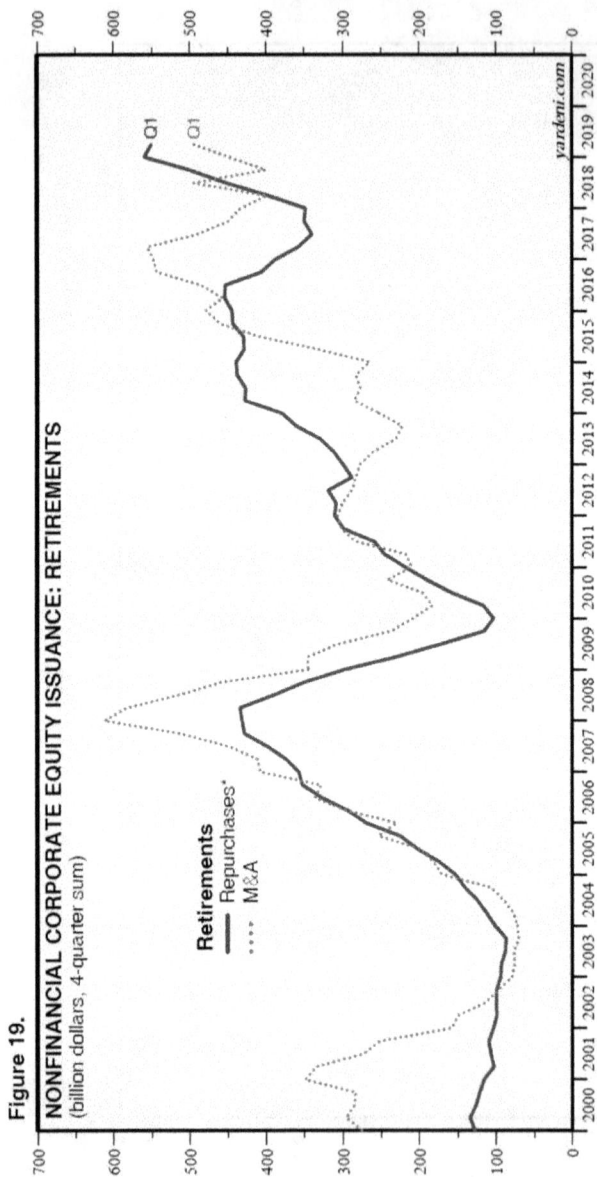

Retirements
—— Repurchases*
····· M&A

Q1

Q1

yardeni.com

* Mostly attributable to S&P 500 buybacks by nonfinancial corporations.
Source: Federal Reserve Board Financial Accounts of the United States.

Figure 20.

NONFINANCIAL CORPORATE EQUITY ISSUANCE: IPO & SEO*
(billion dollars, 12-month sum)

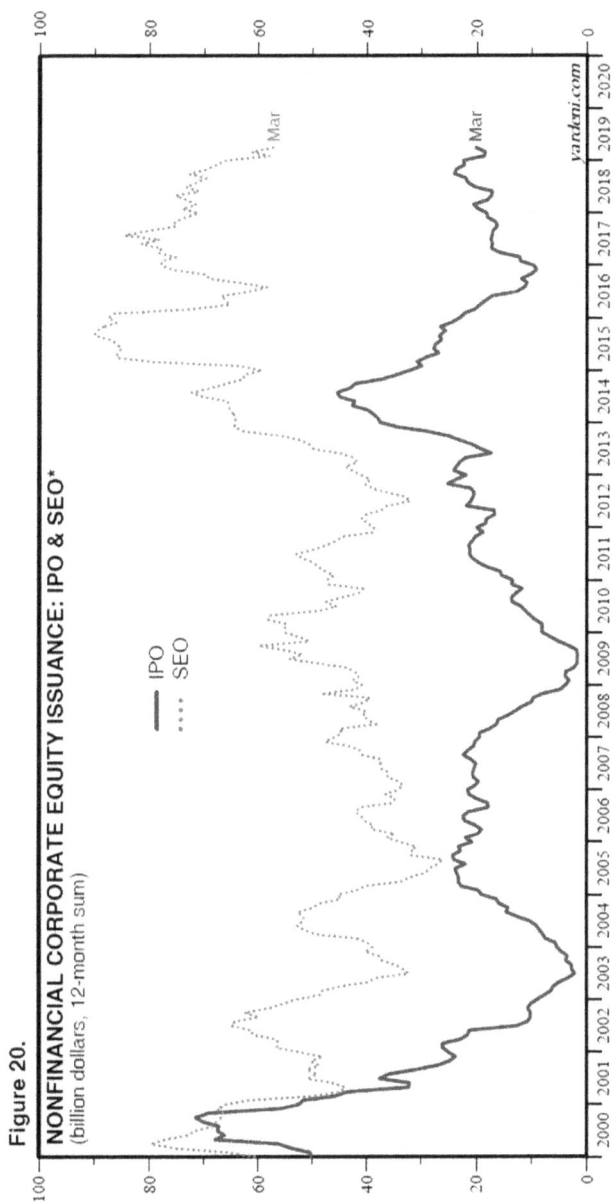

IPO
SEO

* IPO = initial public offerings. SEO = seasoned equity offerings.
Source: Federal Reserve Board Financial Accounts of the United States.

Figure 21.

NONFINANCIAL CORPORATE EQUITY ISSUANCE: GROSS, IPO, & SEO
(billion dollars, 4-quarter & 12-month sum)

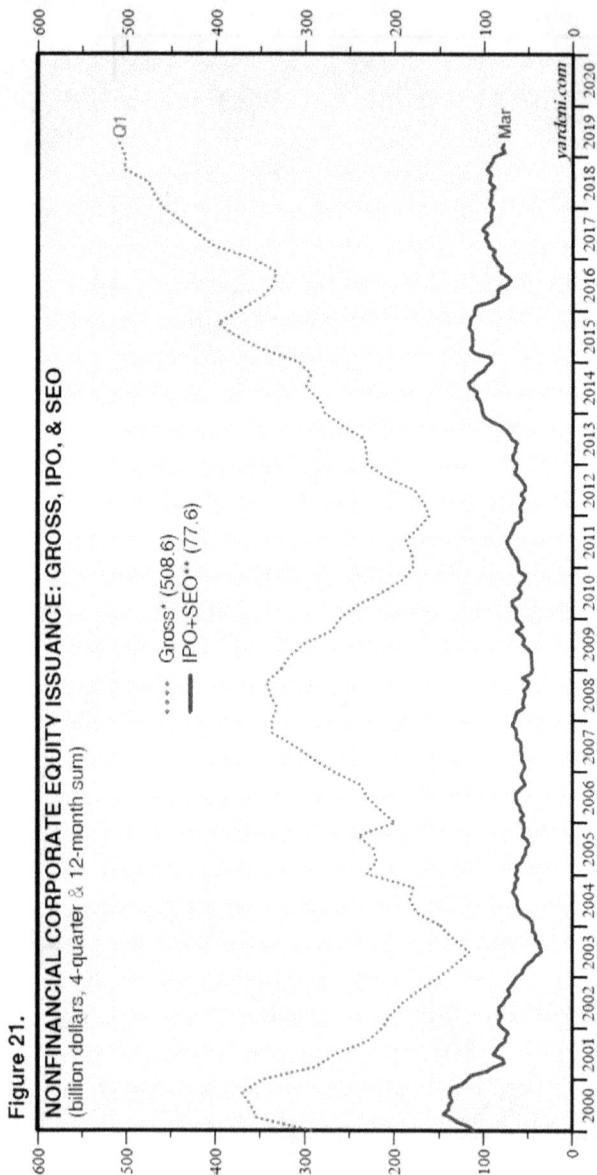

···· Gross* (508.6)
—— IPO+SEO** (77.6)

* Issuance includes initial public offerings, seasoned equity offerings, and private equity. Retirements includes buybacks and M&A activity. Does not include employee stock plans.
** IPO = initial public offerings. SEO = seasoned equity offerings.
Source: Federal Reserve Board Financial Accounts of the United States.

yardeni.com

Figure 22.

S&P 500 DIVIDENDS & BUYBACKS
(trillion dollars, annualized)

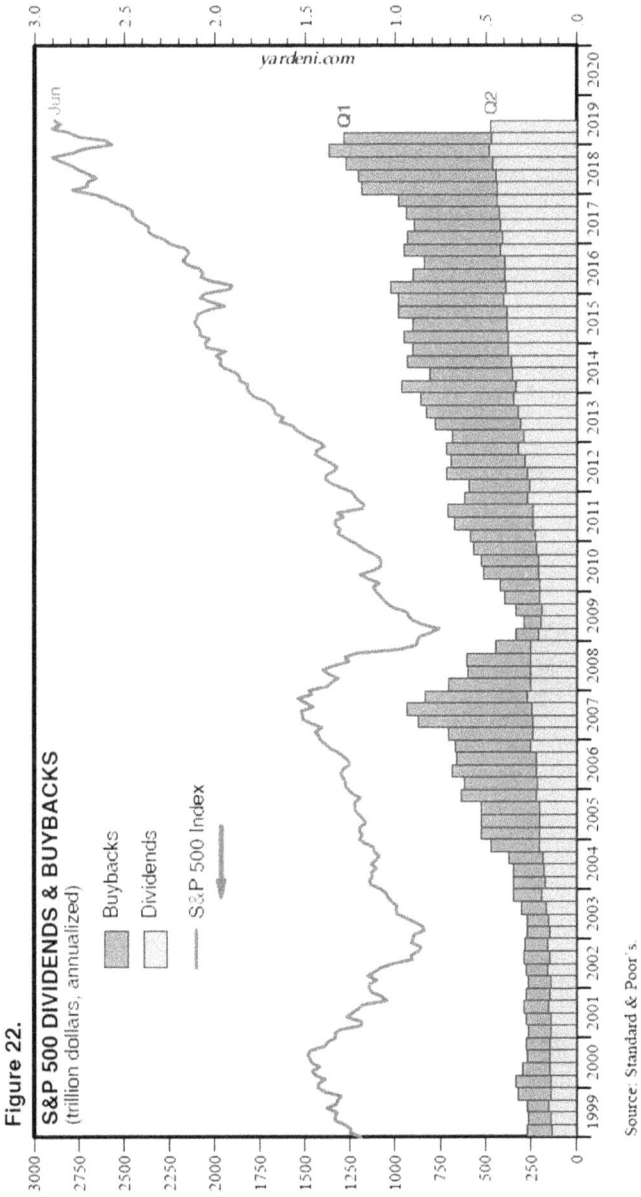

Source: Standard & Poor's.

Figure 23.

S&P 500 BUYBACKS + DIVIDENDS
(as a percent of Operating Earnings)

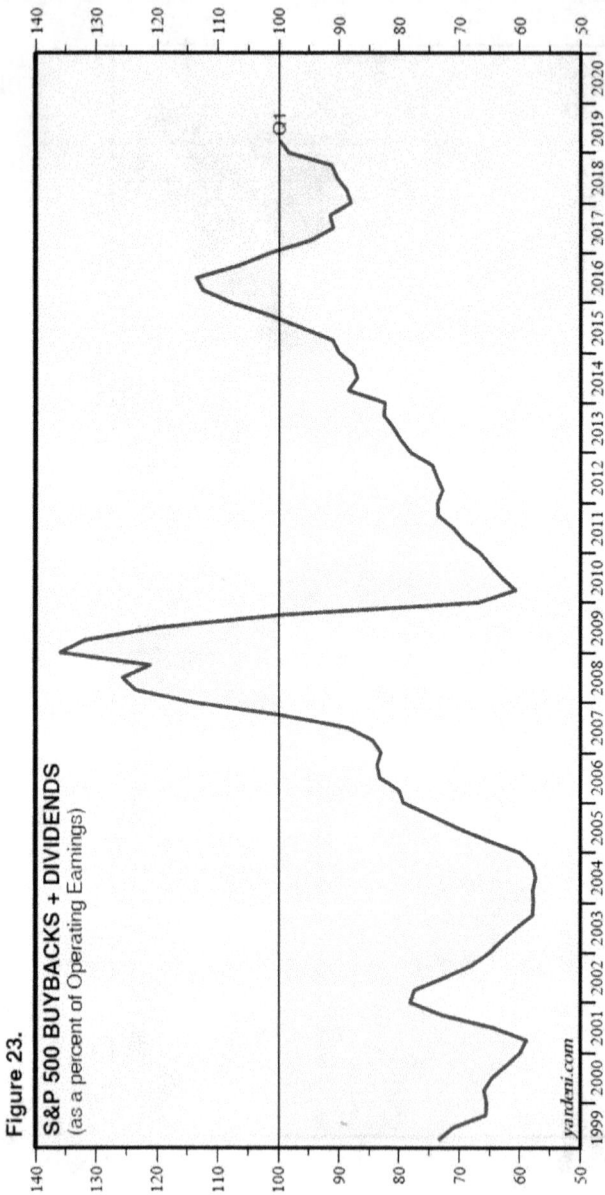

yardeni.com

Source: Standard & Poor's.

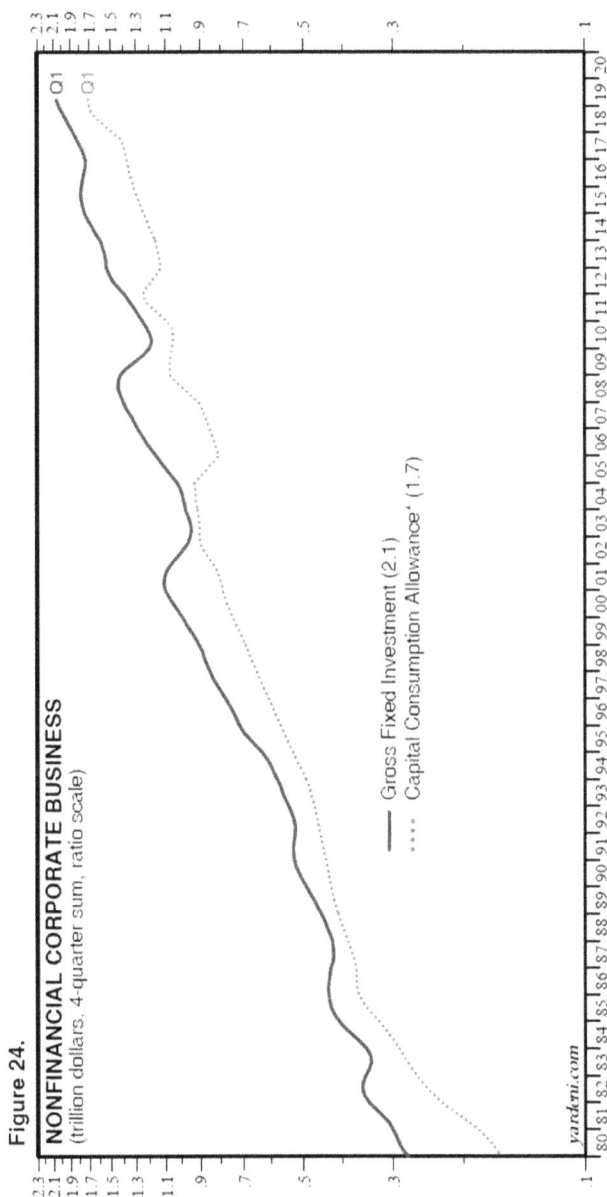

Figure 24.

NONFINANCIAL CORPORATE BUSINESS
(trillion dollars, 4-quarter sum, ratio scale)

—— Gross Fixed Investment (2.1)
······ Capital Consumption Allowance* (1.7)

yardeni.com

* Consumption of fixed capital plus the capital consumption adjustment.
Source: Federal Reserve Board, Financial Accounts of the United States.

Figure 25.

NONFINANCIAL CORPORATE BUSINESS
(billion dollars, 4-quarter sum)

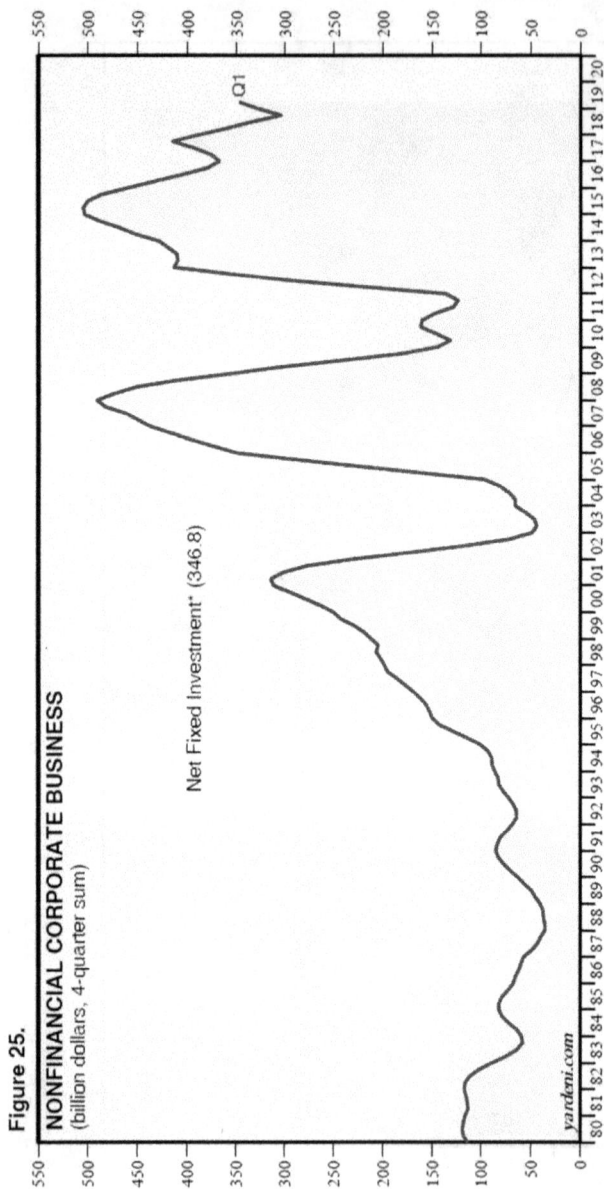

Net Fixed Investment* (346.8)

Q1

yardeni.com

* Gross fixed investment less consumption of fixed capital plus the capital consumption adjustment.
Source: Federal Reserve Board, Financial Accounts of the United States.

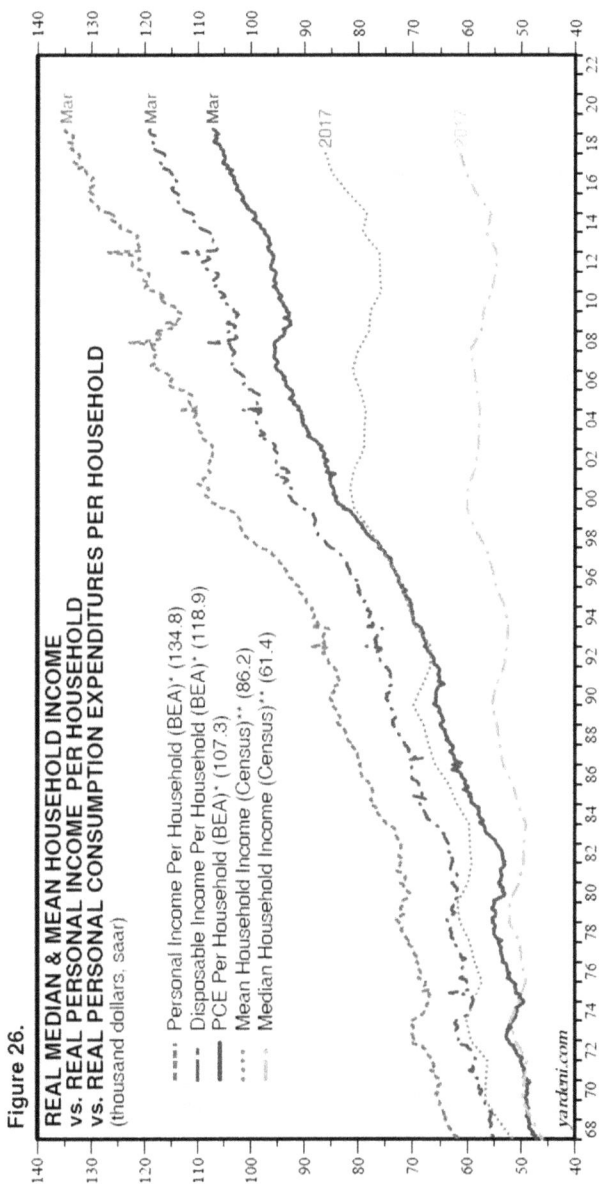

Figure 26.

REAL MEDIAN & MEAN HOUSEHOLD INCOME vs. REAL PERSONAL INCOME PER HOUSEHOLD vs. REAL PERSONAL CONSUMPTION EXPENDITURES PER HOUSEHOLD
(thousand dollars, saar)

- - - Personal Income Per Household (BEA)* (134.8)
— · — Disposable Income Per Household (BEA)* (118.9)
—— PCE Per Household (BEA)* (107.3)
····· Mean Household Income (Census)** (86.2)
— · — Median Household Income (Census)** (61.4)

yardeni.com

* 2009 dollars using PCED **2015 dollars using CPI
Source: Bureau of Economic Analysis, Census Bureau and Current Population Reports.

Figure 27.

REAL AVERAGE HOURLY EARNINGS
PRODUCTION & NONSUPERVISORY WORKERS*
(2012 dollars per hour, ratio scale)

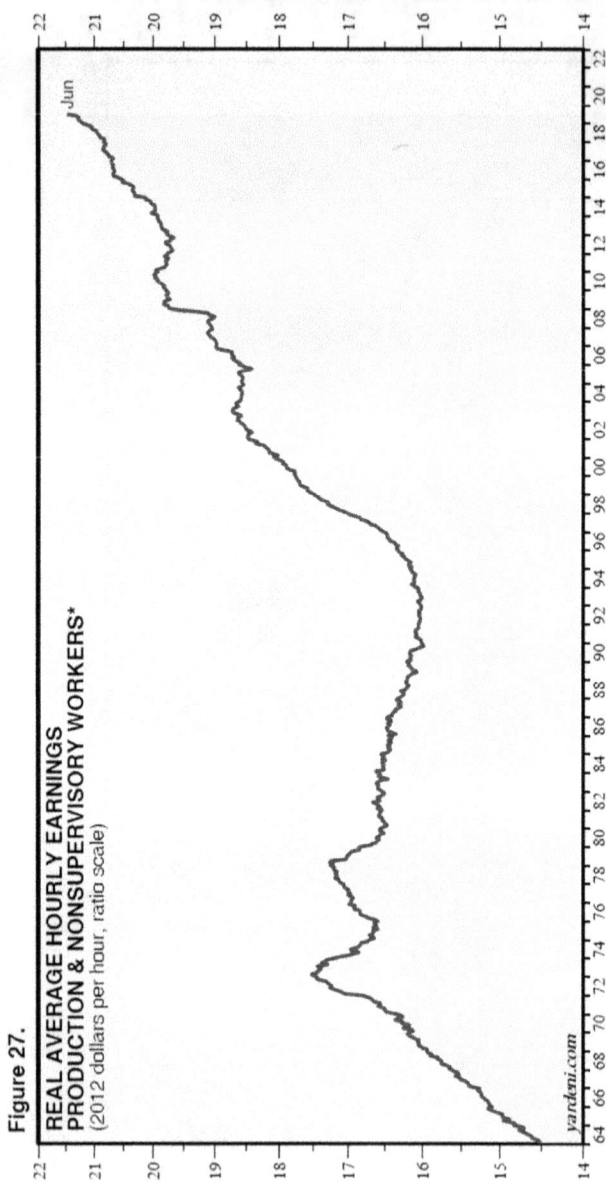

yardeni.com

* Average hourly earnings deflated by personal consumption expenditures deflator.
Source: Bureau of Labor Statistics, Bureau of Economic Analysis, and Haver Analytics.

Figure 28.

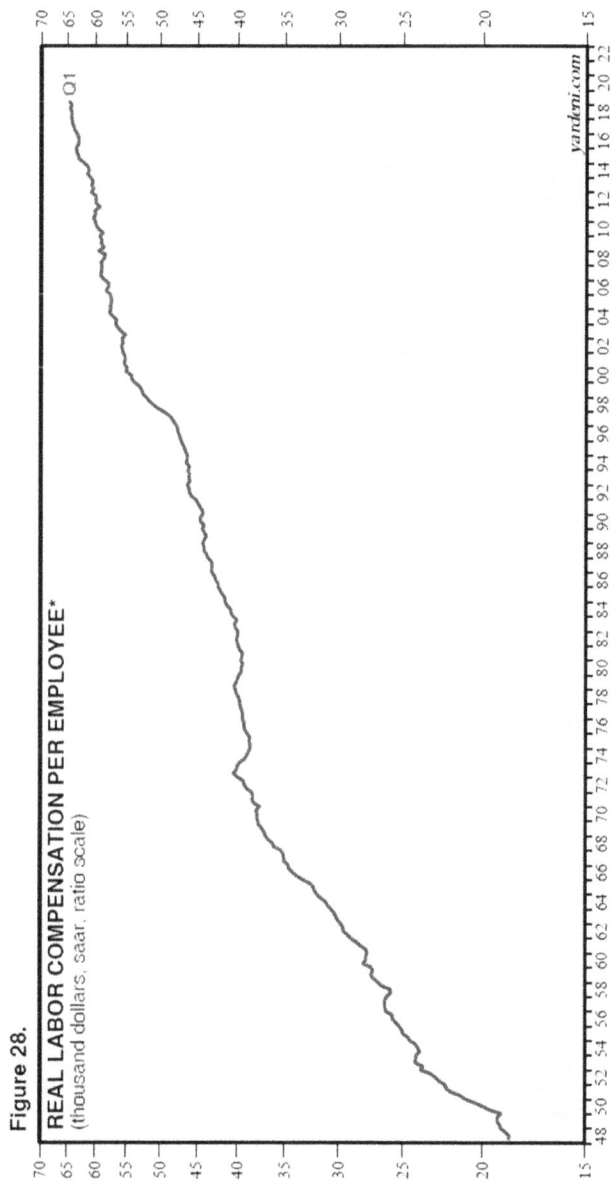

REAL LABOR COMPENSATION PER EMPLOYEE*
(thousand dollars, saar, ratio scale)

yardeni.com

* Total inflation-adjusted wages, salaries, and benefits (using PCE deflator) divided by the household measure of employment
Source: Bureau of Economic Analysis.

Figure 29.

S&P 500 INFORMATION TECHNOLOGY
TOTAL SHARES OUTSTANDING vs S&P 500 DIVISOR

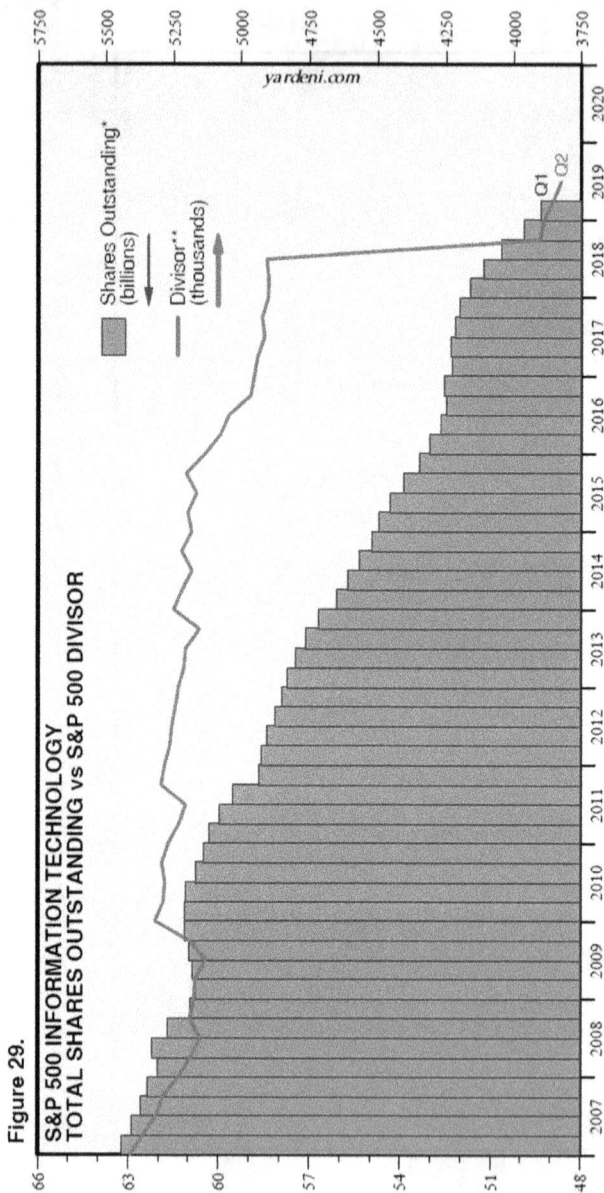

* Total basic shares outstanding (billions) for current S&P 500 companies with data for all periods and adjusted for stock splits and stock dividends.
** Divisor is used to ensure that changes in shares outstanding, capital actions, and the addition or deletion of stocks to the index do not change the level of the index.

Source: Yardeni Research, I/B/E/S data by Refinitiv, and Standard & Poor's.

Figure 30.

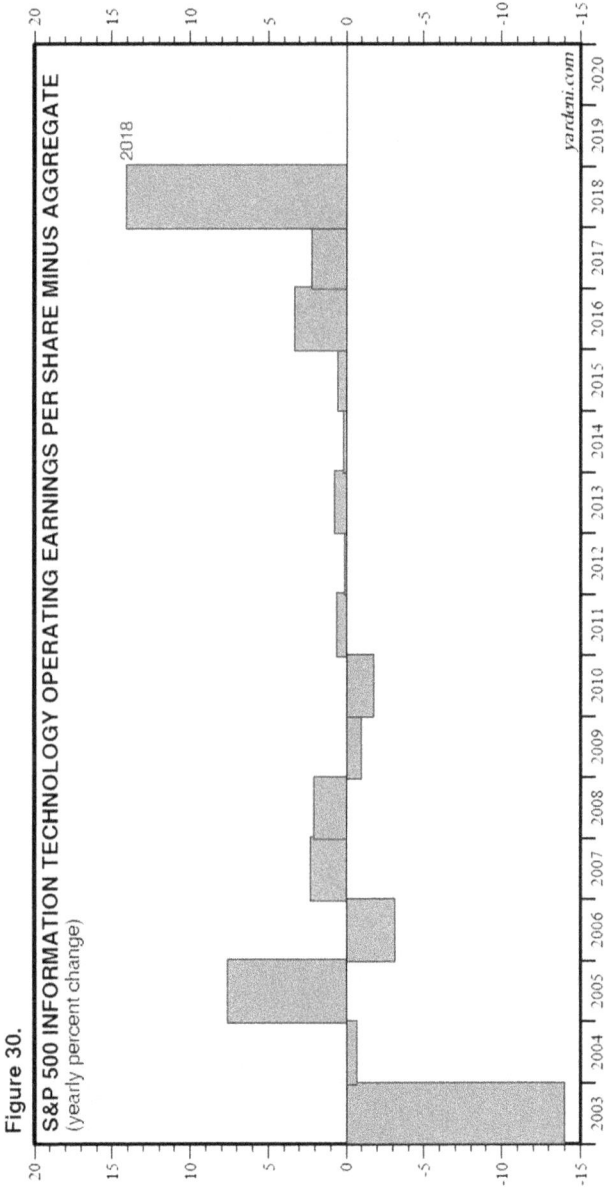

S&P 500 INFORMATION TECHNOLOGY OPERATING EARNINGS PER SHARE MINUS AGGREGATE
(yearly percent change)

Source: Standard & Poor's.

yardeni.com

Figure 31.

S&P 500 INFORMATION TECHNOLOGY IMPLIED AVERAGE PRICE PER SHARE*
(dollars)

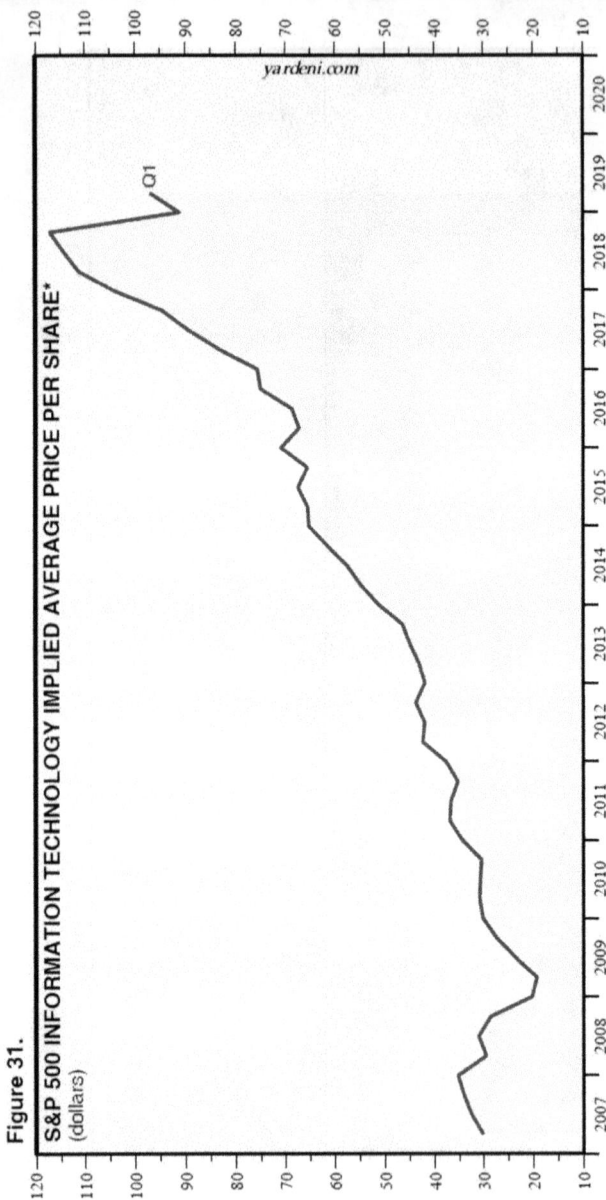

yardeni.com

Q1

* Derived using daily averages for each quarter of market capitalization for S&P 500 divided by basic shares outstanding for all S&P 500 companies at the end of each quarter.
Source: Yardeni Research and I/B/E/S data by Refinitiv.

Figure 32.

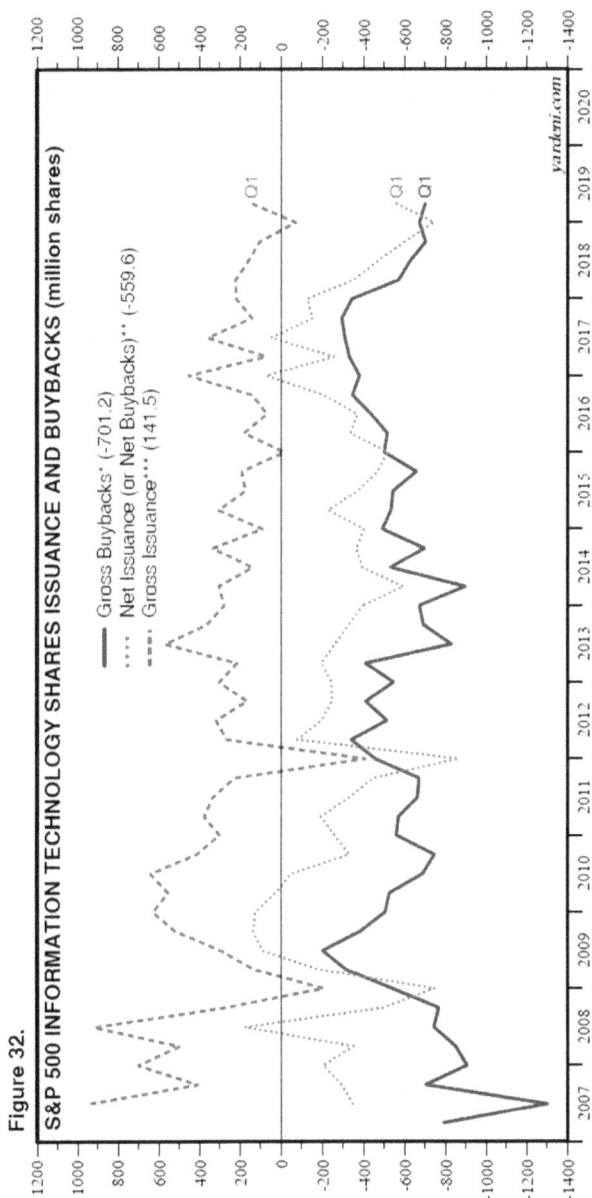

S&P 500 INFORMATION TECHNOLOGY SHARES ISSUANCE AND BUYBACKS (million shares)

—— Gross Buybacks* (-701.2)
········ Net Issuance (or Net Buybacks)** (-559.6)
— — Gross Issuance*** (141.5)

*   Series compiled using S&P's total buybacks and YRI's basic shares outstanding for all S&P 500 Tech companies at the end of each quarter.
**   Series derived by YRI using quarterly changes in basic shares outstanding for all S&P 500 Tech companies at the end of each quarter.
***   Series derived by YRI as Net Issuance + Gross Buybacks.
Source: Yardeni Research and I/B/E/S data by Refinitiv.

Figure 33.

S&P 500 INFORMATION TECHNOLOGY NET BUYBACKS* AS PERCENT OF GROSS BUYBACKS**
(using 4-quarter sums)

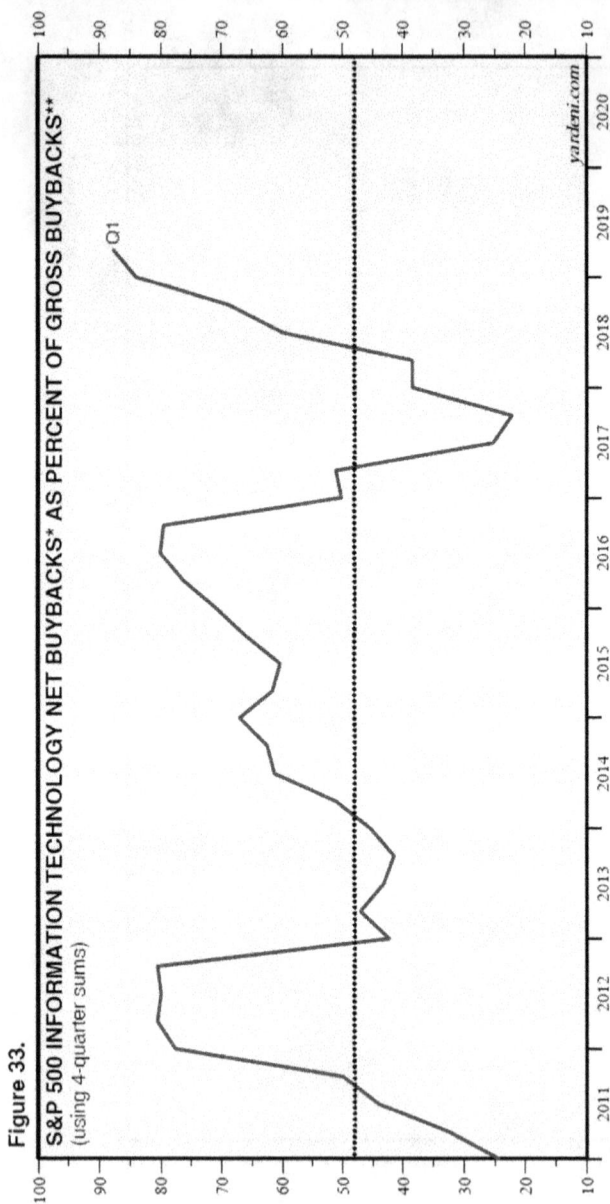

yardeni.com

* Series derived by YRI using quarterly changes in basic shares outstanding for all S&P 500 Tech companies at the end of each quarter.
** Series compiled by S&P.
Source: Yarden Research and I/B/E/S data by Refinitiv.

Figure 34.

S&P 500 NET BUYBACKS* AS PERCENT OF GROSS BUYBACKS**
(using 4-quarter sums)

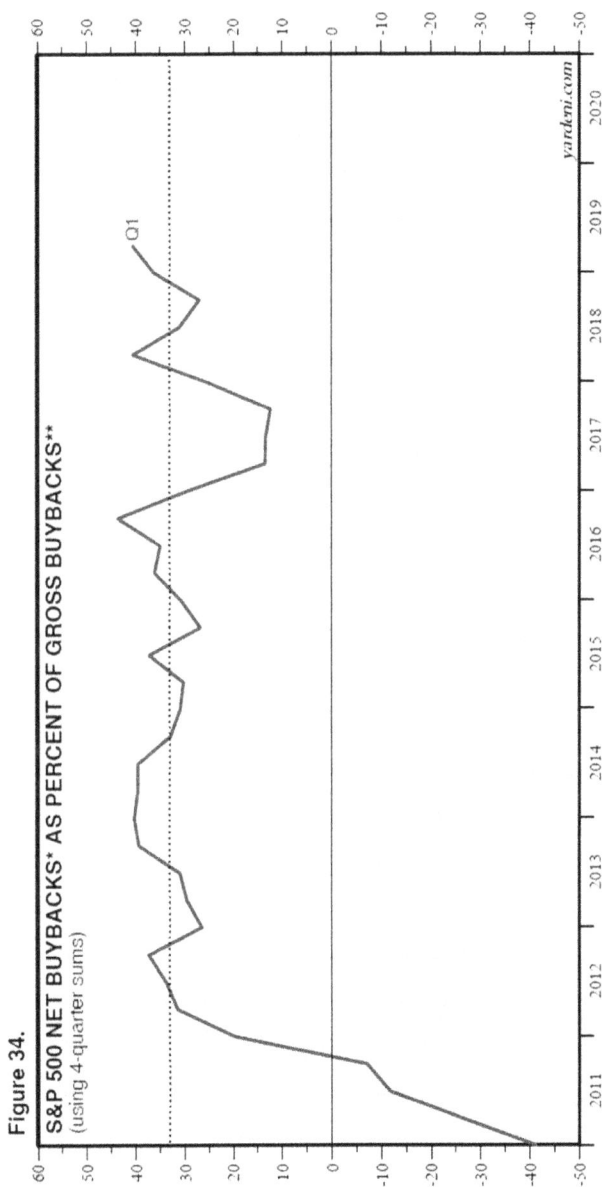

* Series derived by YRI using quarterly changes in basic shares outstanding for all S&P 500 companies at the end of each quarter.
** Series compiled by S&P.
Source: Yardeni Research and I/B/E/S data by Refinitiv.

yardeni.com

Figure 35.

BASIC SHARES OUTSTANDING: AMERICAN EXPRESS
(millions, quarterly)

Latest Basic Shares Outstanding (847.0)

(yearly percent change)

Source: I/B/E/S data by Refinitiv.

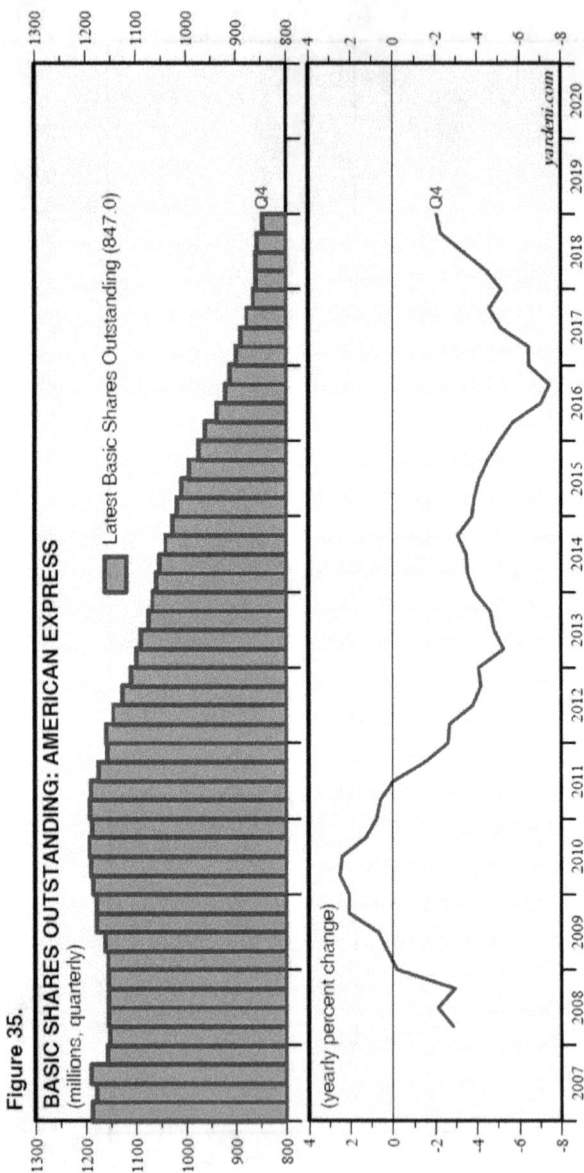

Figure 36.

S&P 500 SHARES OUTSTANDING: BASIC & FULLY DILUTED
(quarterly, billion shares)

Basic (274.7)
Fully Diluted (277.7)

(percent potential dilution)

yardeni.com

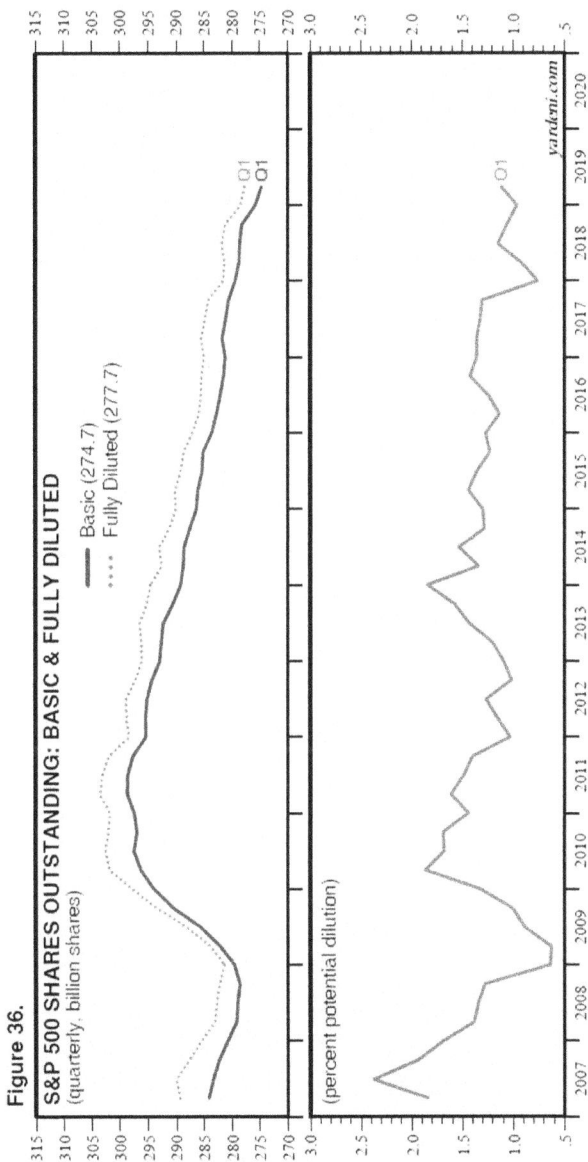

* Total shares outstanding for current S&P 500 companies with data for all periods and adjusted for stock splits and stock dividends.
Source: Yardeni Research and I/B/E/S data by Refinitiv.